MORE PASTA PRESTO

MORE PASTA PRESTO

100 Fast and Fabulous Pasta Sauces

NORMAN KOLPAS

CB

CONTEMPORARY BOOKS

Library of Congress Cataloging-in-Publication Data

Kolpas, Norman.
    More pasta presto : 100 fast and fabulous sauces / Norman Kolpas.
       p.   cm.
    Includes index.
    ISBN 0-8092-3082-8
    1. Sauces.   2. Cookery (Pasta)   I. Title.
TX819.A1K623   1997
641.8'22—dc21   97-22005
                                            CIP

Cover design by Kim Bartko
Cover photograph copyright © Chris Cassidy
Interior design by Nancy Freeborn

Published by Contemporary Books
An imprint of NTC/Contemporary Publishing Company
4255 West Touhy Avenue, Lincolnwood (Chicago), Illinois 60646-1975 U.S.A.
Copyright © 1998 by Norman Kolpas
Printed in the United States of America
International Standard Book Number: 0-8092-3082-8

18   17   16   15   14   13   12   11   10   9   8   7   6   5   4   3   2   1

CONTENTS

PREFACE . . . . *vii*

ACKNOWLEDGMENTS . . . . *ix*

INTRODUCTION *1*

   A Quick Guide to Pasta *1*

   Cooking Pasta *5*

   A Note on Cooking Times *6*

   The Pasta Presto Pantry *6*

   A Note for Vegetarians *10*

1. SEAFOOD SAUCES *11*

2. POULTRY AND MEAT SAUCES *39*

3. VEGETABLE SAUCES *71*

4. DAIRY AND OIL SAUCES *107*

INDEX *129*

REFACE

As a book with the word *presto* in its title demands, these introductory words must be brief.

I like to think that *Pasta Presto*, published in 1988 and the first book I ever wrote on the subject, played some part in the blossoming of our nationwide love affair with pasta. Certainly, countless people have told me they rely on its recipes for fast, delicious meals, and sales are closing in on 200,000 copies—an unbelievable figure for most cookbooks.

Those facts explain the reasons behind *More Pasta Presto*. In short, people can't get enough of good pasta recipes, and many home cooks have asked me for more of the quick, easy kind that characterized that first book.

If anything, this volume aims to go that first title one better. Many of the recipes were developed not merely on the original *Pasta Presto* premise that you would need 30 minutes or less to prepare them but with the added premise that *you can actually make the sauce in less time than it takes you to cook the pasta.*

In that respect, an even more accurate title for this sequel might be *More Presto Pasta*!

ACKNOWLEDGMENTS

The people at Contemporary Books continue to offer great support. My thanks go to everyone connected with the project, including Nancy Crossman, who initiated it; Gerilee Hundt, who saw it through to its conclusion; and Kim Bartko, Tina Chapman, Gigi Grajdura, Maureen Musker, Audrey Sails, Terry Stone, and Kathy Willhoite.

I cook pasta sauces and serve them to my family and friends so often that it would take more than a page of acknowledgments to thank all the "guinea pigs" for the recipes in this book. Above all, however, my thanks go to my wife, Katie, and our son, Jacob, for their support—and for their eternal love of pasta.

INTRODUCTION

A QUICK GUIDE TO PASTA

When you're looking to make a meal in a jiffy, the last thing you want to do is have to search for some specific, and possibly obscure, variety of pasta called for in a recipe. That is why, when you scan the ingredients lists of the recipes in this book, you'll see that each simply calls for "pasta."

Take a closer look, however, at the last line of the introductory notes for each recipe and you'll find some more specific information, along the order of "Serve with medium-width ribbons such as fettuccine or tagliatelle or with bite-sized shapes such as bow ties or fusilli." The reasons for giving such recommendations are twofold: to specify precise pasta types for those cooks who would like them, and to offer more general guidelines for people who would prefer to make their own pasta decisions.

The principles behind all these recommendations are quite simple. Generally, pasta sauces that are lighter or more delicate in flavor or consistency are best suited to pastas that are more delicate in size or shape. Think, for example, of a light tomatoey sauce with thin strands such as angel hair.

Conversely, the more robust a sauce is, the larger the pasta strand, ribbon, or shape it should be served with. Thick, creamy sauces, for example, are shown off best with wider ribbons to which they can cling, while sauces with bite-sized chunks of food in them pair well with pasta shapes of comparable size.

Use the following categories and descriptions to guide you in your own selections of the literally dozens of different pastas you'll find nowadays on the shelves of well-stocked supermarkets. Keep several types from each category on hand so you'll have a good variety of choices for any pasta meal you might decide to make on the spur of the moment.

Strands

Angel hair. Extrafine strands. In Italian, *capelli d'angelo.*

Bavette. Spaghetti-like strands, slightly flattened to an oval in cross section.

Bucatini. Resembles thin spaghetti, with a hole through the center.

Capellini. Common Italian name for fine angel hair strands.

Fedellini. Very thin spaghetti, often cut short and slightly curved.

Fusilli. "Fuses." Thin, squiggly strands. (The term also applies to shorter fuselike shapes.)

Perciatelli. Like bucatini but twice as thick.

Spaghetti. The familiar strings of pasta.

Spaghettini. A thinner version of spaghetti.

Vermicelli. "Little worms." Very thin spaghetti.

Ribbons

Fettuccelli. Narrow form of fettuccine.

Fettucci. Ribbons about ½ inch wide.

Fettuccine. The most familiar ribbons, about ¼ inch wide.

Lasagne. Long ribbons 2 to 3 inches wide, usually layered with fillings and baked.

Linguine. Narrow, thick ribbons that look like flattened spaghetti.

Mafalde. Wide, ripple-edged ribbons.

Mezze lasagne. Narrow, ripple-edged ribbons about twice as wide as fettucine.

Pappardelle. Wide, short ribbons.

Tagliarini. Small, thin tagliatelle.

Tagliatelle. Similar to but somewhat wider than fettuccine.

Tagliolini. Ribbons so narrow they almost resemble spaghetti.

Shapes

Bocconcini. Grooved tubes about 1½ inches long and ½ inch wide.

Bow ties. Shapes resembling bow ties or butterflies (*farfalle* in Italian). Size varies, but the most common are about 2 inches wide.

Cannolicci. Small, ridged tubes.

Cavatappi. Resembling elongated, coiled macaroni tubes.

Cavatelli. Narrow shells with rippled surfaces.

Conchiglie. Conch shells of varying sizes, which are sometimes grooved.

Ditalli. Short macaroni tubes.

Farfalle. "Butterflies," similar to bow ties.

Fusilli. Bite-sized, fuselike shapes about 1 inch long.

Gemelli. "Twins." Two short, intertwined strands.

Gnocchi. Small dumplinglike shapes.

Lumachi. Small snail-shaped shells.

Macaroni. Any pasta tube, but most commonly the short, small to medium-sized, curved tubes known as elbow macaroni.

Maltagliati. Triangles 1 to 2 inches long.

Maruzze. Small to large shells of varying sizes, either smooth or ridged.

Mezzani. Tubes 1 to 2 inches in length.

Mostaccioli. "Little mustaches." Medium-sized tubes about 2 inches long, sometimes grooved, with diagonally cut ends, which are similar to penne.

Orecchiette. "Little ears." Circular indented disks about ½ inch in diameter.

Orzo. Small pasta of the same size and shape as rice.

Penne. "Quill pens." Short, narrow tubes, either smooth or ridged (*rigati*), with diagonally cut ends.

Quadrucci. Small squares, about the size of a fingernail.

Radiatore. "Radiators." Bite-sized shapes resembling heating grills, about 1 inch square.

Rigatoni. Large grooved tubes.

Rotelli. Corkscrew spirals about 1 inch long.

Wagon wheels. Circular shapes with spokes and hubs (*ruote* in Italian), about 1 inch in diameter.

Ziti. Small macaroni-like tubes cut into short or long lengths.

COOKING PASTA

Every recipe in this book specifies the point at which you should start cooking the pasta relative to your cooking of the other ingredients. Any pasta's cooking time will depend upon how thick and how dry it is, and virtually all manufacturers today include suggested cooking times on their packaging. Please refer to these times for any pasta you cook, and follow these basic guidelines:

- **Big pot, lots of water.** Use a large pot filled with a large quantity of water proportionate to the amount of pasta you are cooking. To cook properly, pasta needs plenty of room to circulate freely in the water.

- **Salt and oil?** Some people like to add a little salt to the water, presumably to bring it to a boil faster and to season the pasta; others might add a splash of olive oil to coat the pasta and prevent it from sticking. Neither step is essential, but both may be done if you like.

- **The goal: al dente.** The Italian term *al dente*, meaning "to the tooth" or "chewy," describes pasta that is perfectly cooked, tender but still pleasantly chewy. To test pasta for doneness, use a long fork or slotted spoon to fish a piece out of the boiling water at the earliest cooking time specified in the manufacturer's package instructions. Blow on the pasta to cool it. Then carefully bite into it. If the pasta feels tender enough while still being chewy, and it doesn't have any pale dots of uncooked flour at its center, it is done.

- **Draining and tossing pasta with sauce.** Many people (even I!) make the mistake of draining pasta thoroughly, transferring it to serving bowls or plates, and ladling sauce on top. More often than not, this leads to pasta that is less than hot by the time you eat it and that has begun to stick together. The solution is to drain pasta quickly and instantly toss it, still glistening with water, with the sauce. Italians will even do this over low heat in the pot in which the sauce or the pasta cooked. Sometimes, a splash of the pasta's cooking water is even added to help pasta and sauce mix together.

A Note on Cooking Times

Throughout this book, you'll see that I try not only to specify cooking times for each stage of a recipe but also to relate those times to sensory clues—taste, aroma, sight, touch, even hearing—that tell you when the ingredients are ready for the next step. Train yourself to rely on your own senses rather than on the clock and more likely than not you'll find that your cooking magically improves.

The Pasta Presto Pantry

In addition to the pasta varieties already discussed, it's a good idea to have on hand in your kitchen pantry or cupboard and refrigerator a number of basic ingredients that will guarantee you the ability to put together a great pasta meal in a matter of minutes. Here's a brief review of those used in this book.

Butter

Unsalted (sweet) butter has a fresher, purer flavor than the salted kind and lets *you* decide how much salt to add to a recipe to suit your own tastes. Every market carries it. Keep a good supply on hand, storing any excess in your freezer.

Cheeses

From good-quality imported Italian Parmesan, bought in block form and grated fresh when needed, to fresh domestic goat cheese, cheese is an indispensable element of many pasta meals. You will find all the cheeses called for in this book with ease in the dairy sections of well-stocked supermarkets. Store them in the refrigerator wrapped in plastic wrap.

Cream

Used as an occasional splurge, heavy cream or, less often, half-and-half lusciously enriches pasta dishes. Be sure to buy cartons of fresh pasteurized cream, avoiding those products that have been ultraheat treated.

Eggs

With the rare exception of the classic egg-enriched dish Pasta Carbonara, most people don't instantly think of pasta and eggs as going together. Yet, a number of very satisfying, exceedingly quick pasta dishes may be made with eggs (see Index). Use extra-large eggs for the recipes in this book.

Garlic

So many Italian-inspired pasta sauces gain an extra dimension from the heady taste of garlic. Buy it in whole heads and store in a dry, airy place. For a change of pace, also seek out jars of roasted garlic cloves packed in olive oil, which have a rich, sweet, mellow flavor; you'll find them in well-stocked supermarkets and specialty food stores.

Herbs

You'll find all the dried herbs called for in this book in the seasonings aisle of any supermarket. In addition, many of the recipes require fresh herbs, which you can find in farmers' markets, produce stands, or the produce departments of well-stocked supermarkets. You can also easily grow them yourself in your backyard, on your patio, or on a sunny windowsill.

Fresh basil, in particular, is one of the most popular fresh herbs for pasta, particularly in the form of the **Genovese classic basil pesto sauce**. Instead of repeating the very popular pesto recipe from *Pasta Presto* in the recipe chapters of this book, I give it here as a bonus in an abbreviated form: Put 3 cups packed fresh stemmed basil leaves, 1½ cups extra-virgin olive oil, 1 cup grated Parmesan, ¾ cup toasted pine nuts, and 4 peeled garlic cloves in a food processor fitted with the metal blade. Turn the machine on and off rapidly several times to chop the ingredients coarse. Scrape down the work bowl. Then process continuously until the sauce is smooth, pulsing in a little hot water if the sauce seems too thick. Makes about 2½ cups. Serves 4 to 6.

Nuts

Nutmeats of various kinds add crunchy texture and rich flavor to pasta sauces, as well as contributing body to pureed pestos. Buy nuts in bulk, if you like, and store them in airtight bags in your freezer. To toast nuts, thus developing their taste and crispness, spread them evenly in a single layer on a foil-lined baking sheet and bake in a 450°F oven until light golden, 3 to 10 minutes, depending on the size and type of nut. Watch carefully to guard against scorching. The nuts will continue to darken slightly after you take them from the oven.

Olive Oil

The incomparably fruity, rich flavor of olive oil lends distinction to many pasta dishes, whether on its own or as the cooking base for tomatoes and other compatible ingredients. Use extra-virgin olive oil, extracted on the first pressing from ripe olives without the use of heat or chemicals. It has a pure, aromatic flavor and a bright color that, depending on the olives and on how the oil was filtered, may range from pale golden to deep green. Generally, the darker the oil, the more pronounced the flavor. Store olive oil, and all other cooking oils, in an airtight container away from light and heat.

Peppers

Both sweet bell peppers and hot chili peppers add sparks of color and flavor to many pasta sauces. Roasting intensifies their flavor and gives them a supple, tender texture while loosening their hard-to-digest skins. You can find jars of roasted peppers in well-stocked supermarkets or specialty food stores. To roast them yourself, place the peppers on a foil-lined baking sheet in a 500°F oven. Roast until evenly blistered and browned, 15 to 25 minutes, depending on size, turning the peppers several times so they'll roast evenly. Remove from the oven, cover with a kitchen towel, and leave until cool enough to handle. Then, pull out the stems, peel away the blackened skins, open up the peppers, and remove their seeds. (Note: When working with hot chilies, take care to avoid touching your eyes or any other sensitive areas, wearing gloves if you have any cuts on your hands. Chilies contain fiery oils that can cause painful burning sensations. Be sure to wash your hands thoroughly with lots of warm, soapy water after handling them.)

Shallots

Thought by some people to resemble in taste a cross between onions and garlic, these smallish, brown-skinned, purplish-fleshed bulbs are available with increasing frequency in well-stocked supermarkets. Peel and chop them as you would onions.

Sun-Dried Tomatoes

When dried in the sunshine or in a kiln or oven, tomatoes develop a chewy consistency and an intensely tangy-sweet flavor, both of which can easily add extra dimension to a pasta dish when used as a featured ingredient or garnish. You can buy sun-dried tomatoes packed in olive oil, which keeps them supple and chewy, or air-packed in plastic bags. The latter, though lower in fat, of course, have a less complex flavor. They also require rehydrating before use in a recipe, by covering them with warm tap water for 10 to 15 minutes or until soft.

Tomato Paste Concentrate

This thick, deep red paste goes a long way toward enhancing the flavor of tomato-based pasta sauces. Ever since I first started developing the recipes for my first pasta book, *Pasta Presto*, I have been a devotee of tubes of double-strength tomato paste concentrate imported from Italy. Not only is the product's flavor better and more intense than regular tomato paste, but the tubes are also more convenient than cans, since they reseal with a twist-on cap like a tube of toothpaste and can be stored easily in the refrigerator. You'll find these in well-stocked supermarkets, specialty food stores, and Italian delicatessens. In a pinch, you can use regular canned tomato paste, adding twice the quantity called for in the recipe.

Tomatoes

Some of the recipes in this book call for fresh Roma tomatoes, which as a rule are your best bet for flavor year-round. These egg-shaped tomatoes are also known as Italian plum tomatoes. At the height of the summer, by all means substitute other, sun-ripened varieties, if available. Or you may simply use plain canned tomatoes, avoiding seasoned products. For rapid sauces, I particularly like the convenience of diced or crushed tomatoes over canned whole tomatoes, as they break down more quickly and easily during cooking.

A Note for Vegetarians

Pasta is an ideal dish for the vegetarian or vegan lifestyle, and many of the recipes in this book fit in perfectly with such eating plans. You'll find vegetarian and vegan recipes clearly marked in the listings on pages 71–72 and 107–108.

Seafood Sauces

Baby Bay Shrimp with Lemon-Dill Butter

Grilled Shrimp with Lime-Ginger Butter

Baby Bay Shrimp with Bacon and Chives

Grilled Shrimp with Ginger-Champagne Cream and Caviar

Grilled Scallops with Pancetta and Sun-Dried Tomatoes

Grilled Scallops with Ginger-Soy Butter

Spicy and Zesty Crab

Anchovy Butter

Spicy Steamed Clams with Fresh Tomatoes and Garlic

Quick White Clam Sauce with Pancetta

Mussels with Coconut Cream

Spicy Anchovy Butter with Roasted Garlic

Anchovy Pissaladière

Sardines, Tomato, and Fresh Dill

Smoked Salmon, Roma Tomatoes, Capers, and Lemon Zest

Grilled Salmon with Tomato Cream and Arugula

Smoked Salmon with Vodka Cream

Smoked Salmon with Garlic-Herb Cheese

*Smoked Salmon, Smoked Trout, Golden Caviar,
and Lemon-Orange Butter*

Tuna Caponata

Tuna, Olives, Garlic, and Fresh Herbs

Tuna with Celery

Tuna with Spring Peas

BABY BAY SHRIMP
WITH LEMON-DILL BUTTER

Sweet and tender, little precooked baby bay shrimp—sold in the fresh seafood section of most well-stocked markets—are a real asset to the quick pasta maker. All they need in this particular recipe to highlight their flavor is a quick tossing with butter, lemon juice, and dill just before the pasta is done.

Serve with fine to medium-width strands such as angel hair, spaghetti, or linguine or with small shells.

¾ pound pasta

1 cup (2 sticks) unsalted butter,
    cut into pieces

1 pound cooked bay shrimp

¼ cup finely chopped fresh dill

2 tablespoons lemon juice

Salt

White pepper

Bring a large pot of water to a boil. Add the pasta and cook until al dente, following the manufacturer's suggested cooking time.

A few minutes before the pasta is done, melt the butter in a large skillet over medium-low heat. Add the shrimp and cook until heated through, 1 to 2 minutes. Stir in the dill and lemon juice and season to taste with salt and white pepper.

As soon as the pasta is done, drain it and toss well with the sauce. Serve immediately.

 SERVES 4 TO 6

GRILLED SHRIMP WITH LIME-GINGER BUTTER

Restaurateur Michael McCarty, owner of Michael's restaurants in Santa Monica and New York, introduced me to the delicious flavor combination of lime and ginger, which goes so well with fresh seafood. If you wish, substitute grilled scallops for the shrimp.

Serve with thin strands such as angel hair or spaghettini.

¾ pound pasta

1 cup (2 sticks) unsalted butter, cut into pieces

2 shallots, chopped fine

18 jumbo shrimp, peeled and deveined

Salt

White pepper

3 tablespoons lime juice

1 tablespoon finely grated peeled fresh ginger

2 tablespoons finely chopped fresh cilantro leaves

Preheat a grill or broiler.

Bring a large pot of water to a boil. Add the pasta and cook until al dente, following the manufacturer's suggested cooking time.

As soon as the pasta starts cooking, melt the butter with the shallots in a large skillet over medium heat.

Brush the shrimp with a little of the butter, season them lightly with salt and white pepper, and grill or broil them until they turn pink, opaque, and lightly golden but still juicy, about 2 minutes per side.

Stir the lime juice and ginger into the melted butter and continue cooking briefly until heated through. Season to taste with salt and white pepper.

As soon as the pasta is done, drain it and toss with the butter mixture. Arrange in individual serving plates or bowls and garnish with cilantro. Serve immediately.

 SERVES 4 TO 6

Baby Bay Shrimp with Bacon and Chives

Like most crustaceans, bay shrimp go especially well with the smoky-sweet taste and crisp edge of bacon. You'll find the precooked shrimp in the fresh seafood section of most well-stocked supermarkets. Use the best-quality, leanest bacon you can find.

Serve with fine to medium-width strands such as angel hair, spaghetti, or linguine or with small shells.

¾ pound pasta

2 tablespoons extra-virgin olive oil

¼ pound thinly sliced smoked bacon, cut crosswise into ¼-inch pieces

¾ cup (1½ sticks) unsalted butter, cut into pieces

¾ pound cooked bay shrimp

2 tablespoons finely chopped fresh chives

2 tablespoons finely chopped fresh Italian parsley

Salt

Black pepper

Grated Parmesan cheese

Bring a large pot of water to a boil. Add the pasta and cook until al dente, following the manufacturer's suggested cooking time.

As soon as the pasta starts cooking, heat the olive oil in a large skillet over medium heat. Add the bacon and cook until it just begins to turn crisp, 3 to 4 minutes.

Pour off most of the fat from the skillet. Add the butter and reduce the heat to low. As soon as the butter melts, stir in the shrimp and cook until heated through, 1 to 2 minutes. Stir in the chives and parsley and season to taste with salt and pepper.

As soon as the pasta is done, drain it and toss well with the sauce. Serve immediately, passing Parmesan for guests to add to taste.

Serves 4 to 6

GRILLED SHRIMP WITH
GINGER-CHAMPAGNE CREAM AND CAVIAR

Here's an Asian-inspired treatment for fresh shrimp over pasta that couldn't be simpler and yet more elegant. Serve it for a special dinner party. You can use fairly inexpensive roes for the caviar, such as orange-pink salmon roe or golden caviar. As an extra, intriguing touch, I suggest garnishing each serving with thin strips of Japanese nori, *the dried sheets of seaweed used to enclose sushi rolls. You can find it in Asian markets or the Asian food section of well-stocked supermarkets; alternatively, use chopped chives.*

✂ *Serve with thin strands such as angel hair or spaghettini.*

6 tablespoons unsalted butter, cut into pieces

18 jumbo shrimp, peeled and deveined

4 shallots, chopped fine

1 cup medium-dry champagne or other sparkling white wine

1 1-inch piece fresh peeled ginger

2 cups heavy cream

¾ pound pasta

Salt

White pepper

2 tablespoons salmon roe or golden caviar (whitefish roe)

¼ cup thinly shredded *nori* or finely chopped fresh chives

Preheat a grill or broiler. Bring a large pot of water to a boil.

Meanwhile, melt the butter in a large skillet or saucepan over medium heat. Put the shrimp in a bowl and drizzle about one-third of the butter over them. Toss to coat them and set aside.

Add the shallots to the remaining butter and sauté until tender, 2 to 3 minutes. Add the champagne and raise the heat to high. Put the ginger in a garlic press and press it over the skillet or pan, letting its juices drip into the pan; alternatively, grate the ginger into the pan. Boil the champagne briskly until it reduces by one-half, 5 to 7 minutes.

Add the cream to the reduced champagne and continue boiling until thick and reduced by one-fourth to one-third, about 10 minutes more.

As soon as you add the cream to the champagne, put the pasta in the boiling water and cook until al dente, following the manufacturer's suggested cooking time.

Season the shrimp lightly with salt and white pepper and grill or broil them until they turn pink, opaque, and lightly golden but still juicy, about 2 minutes per side.

As soon as the pasta is done, drain it and toss with the sauce. Arrange in individual serving plates or bowls and top with the grilled shrimp. Garnish with the salmon roe or golden caviar and the shredded *nori* and serve immediately.

ERVES 4 TO 6

GRILLED SCALLOPS WITH PANCETTA AND SUN-DRIED TOMATOES

This recipe takes inspiration from a very popular way of serving sea scallops, in which the sweet, tender morsels of shellfish are wrapped and cooked in bacon. Here, I call for pancetta, the salt-cured, rolled bacon widely found in Italian delicatessens and well-stocked supermarkets. Buy it cut into thin slices, and then chop it up at home. Alternatively, use good-quality, thinly sliced lean bacon.

Serve with thin to medium-width strands or ribbons such as spaghettini, spaghetti, linguine, or tagliatelle.

1 cup (2 sticks) unsalted butter, cut into pieces

1 pound sea scallops, trimmed

Salt

White pepper

¾ pound pasta

6 ounces pancetta, chopped coarse

6 tablespoons drained sun-dried tomatoes, cut into thin slivers

2 tablespoons thinly shredded fresh basil leaves

1 tablespoon finely chopped fresh chives

SERVES 4 TO 6

Preheat the broiler. Bring a large pot of water to a boil.

In a skillet, melt the butter over medium-low heat. With a basting brush, lightly coat the scallops with a little of the melted butter. Season the scallops to taste with salt and white pepper, place them on a broiler tray, and set them aside.

Put the pasta in the boiling water and cook until al dente, following the manufacturer's suggested cooking time.

As soon as the pasta starts cooking, add the pancetta to the melted butter in the skillet and cook over medium-low heat just until the pancetta pieces start to turn golden, 4 to 5 minutes. Add the sun-dried tomatoes, stir, and cook about 1 minute more. Cover, set aside, and keep warm.

Put the scallops under the broiler and cook them until golden on the outside but still juicy within, 1 to 2 minutes per side.

As soon as the pasta is done, drain it and toss with the butter, pancetta, and sun-dried tomatoes, seasoning to taste with a little salt and white pepper. Arrange on individual serving plates or in shallow bowls, top with the grilled scallops, garnish with basil and chives, and serve immediately.

GRILLED SCALLOPS WITH GINGER-SOY BUTTER

Quickly broiled scallops and a simple butter sauce seasoned with ginger and soy yield an elegant main course with an Asian twist. Medium-to-large shrimp may be substituted for the scallops. You can find Japanese rice vinegar in the Asian food section of most well-stocked supermarkets; if it is unavailable, substitute medium-dry sherry.

Serve with medium-width strands or ribbons such as spaghetti, linguine, or fettuccine.

1 cup (2 sticks) plus 2 tablespoons unsalted butter, cut into pieces

¾ pound pasta

1 pound sea scallops, trimmed

Salt

White pepper

¼ cup Japanese seasoned rice vinegar

1½ tablespoons finely grated peeled fresh ginger

1 tablespoon soy sauce

2 tablespoons finely chopped fresh chives

Preheat the broiler. Bring a large pot of water to a boil. In a small saucepan or in the microwave, melt 2 tablespoons of the butter.

Put the pasta in the boiling water and cook until al dente, following the manufacturer's suggested cooking time.

As soon as the pasta starts cooking, brush the scallops with the melted butter and season to taste with salt and white pepper. Place them on a broiler tray and set them aside.

Put the rice vinegar, ginger, and soy sauce in a medium-sized saucepan and cook over medium-high heat until the liquids have reduced by about one-half, 3 to 4 minutes. Reduce the heat to medium-low, add the butter pieces, and swirl the pan until they melt and blend with the other ingredients to form a smooth, thick sauce. Taste the sauce and add salt and white pepper to taste if necessary. Cover to keep warm and set aside.

Put the scallops under the broiler and cook them until golden on the outside but still juicy within, 1 to 2 minutes per side.

As soon as the pasta is done, drain it and toss with the butter sauce. Arrange on individual serving plates or in shallow bowls, top with the grilled scallops, garnish with chives, and serve immediately.

 Serves 4 to 6

SPICY AND ZESTY CRAB

Buy freshly cooked, ready-to-use, shelled lump crabmeat from a good seafood shop or the seafood department of a quality supermarket. Hints of hot chili and tangy lemon zest, along with the melted butter that so often accompanies the crustacean, complement the crab perfectly.

 *Serve with thin to medium-width strands or ribbons such as angel hair, spaghetti, linguine, tagliatelle, or fettuccine.*

¾ pound pasta

1 cup (2 sticks) unsalted butter

½ to 1 teaspoon crushed red pepper flakes

1 pound lump crabmeat, flaked coarse and carefully picked over to remove any pieces of shell or gristle

1 tablespoon grated lemon zest

Salt

White pepper

2 tablespoons finely chopped fresh Italian parsley

Bring a large pot of water to a boil. Add the pasta and cook until al dente, following the manufacturer's suggested cooking time.

A few minutes before the pasta is done, melt the butter in a large skillet over medium-low heat. Stir in red pepper flakes to taste. Then add the crabmeat, stirring gently until heated through, 1 to 2 minutes.

As soon as the pasta is done, drain it and toss with the crab-and-butter mixture and the lemon zest. Season with salt and white pepper to taste. Garnish with parsley and serve immediately.

SERVES 4 TO 6

NCHOVY BUTTER

For anchovy lovers, no pasta sauce could be easier or better tasting. Using a tube of anchovy paste makes the process very easy and the results even more aesthetically pleasing, as you don't have to contend with the fine little bones. Most well-stocked supermarkets carry anchovy paste; if yours does not, you can find it in specialty food stores or delicatessens.

Serve with thin to medium-width strands or ribbons such as spaghettini, spaghetti, linguine, or tagliatelle.

¾ pound pasta

1 cup (2 sticks) unsalted butter, at room temperature

6 tablespoons anchovy paste

2 tablespoons lemon juice

4 tablespoons finely chopped fresh Italian parsley

Grated Parmesan cheese

Bring a large pot of water to a boil. Add the pasta and cook until al dente, following the manufacturer's suggested cooking time.

Meanwhile, put the butter, anchovy paste, and lemon juice in a food processor fitted with the metal blade. Process until smooth, stopping once or twice to scrape down the work bowl. Alternatively, simply use a fork to mash the ingredients together in a small bowl.

As soon as the pasta is done, drain it and toss with the anchovy butter. Garnish with chopped parsley and serve immediately, passing Parmesan for guests to add to taste.

ERVES 4 TO 6

SPICY STEAMED CLAMS WITH FRESH TOMATOES AND GARLIC

For those who love Italian-style red clam sauce, no recipe featuring fresh clams could be simpler. Be sure to get your clams from a reputable fishmonger and buy them only if they have a fresh, clean smell of the sea, with no trace of any off odor.

 *Serve with linguine or spaghetti.*

48 fresh live Manila clams or other small to medium-sized hard-shelled clams

¾ pound pasta

½ cup extra-virgin olive oil

6 cloves garlic, chopped fine

1 to 2 teaspoons crushed red pepper flakes

1 pound Roma tomatoes, cored and chopped coarse

½ tablespoon sugar

2 teaspoons dried oregano

Salt

Black pepper

1 cup dry white wine

Scrub the clams well under cold running water to remove any traces of dirt from their shells. Soak the clams for 30 minutes in a sink or large basin filled with water. Then drain, discarding any whose shells gape open and do not close when tapped.

Bring a large pot of water to a boil. Add the pasta and cook until al dente, following the manufacturer's suggested cooking time.

Meanwhile, in another large pot, heat the olive oil over medium heat. Add the garlic and red pepper flakes and sauté about 1 minute. Add the tomatoes, sugar, and oregano and season to taste with salt and pepper. Cook, stirring frequently, for about 2 minutes. Add the wine and, as soon as it begins to simmer, add the clams. Reduce the heat slightly, cover the pot, and cook until all the shells are open, 3 to 5 minutes more.

Drain the pasta, arrange in a large serving bowl or individual shallow bowls, and spoon the sauce and clams on top, discarding any clams that have not opened. Serve immediately.

Serves 4 to 6

QUICK WHITE CLAM SAUCE WITH PANCETTA

Purist friends of mine sometimes scoff at the use of canned clams for pasta sauces. Sometimes, however, it's just not that easy to get your hands on fresh clams in the shell, and at those times an easy sauce like this satisfies the craving for a taste of the sea. Besides, I really like the way canned clams taste in this sauce!

If you can't find pancetta, the Italian salt-cured bacon sold in well-stocked supermarkets and Italian delicatessens, substitute lean bacon.

Serve with linguine, spaghetti, or other medium-width strands.

¾ pound pasta

4 tablespoons (½ stick) unsalted butter

¼ cup extra-virgin olive oil

4 cloves garlic, chopped fine

¼ pound thinly sliced pancetta, cut into ¼- to ½-inch pieces

1 teaspoon crushed red pepper flakes

2 10¼-ounce cans whole baby clams, drained

¾ cup bottled clam juice

¼ cup heavy cream

¼ cup coarsely chopped fresh Italian parsley

2 tablespoons dried oregano

Salt

Black pepper

Bring a large pot of water to a boil. Add the pasta and cook until al dente, following the manufacturer's suggested cooking time.

Meanwhile, heat the butter, olive oil, garlic, pancetta, and red pepper flakes in a large skillet over medium heat. As soon as the butter melts and the garlic sizzles and begins to give off its aroma, add the clams and sauté about 1 minute more.

Add the clam juice, cream, parsley, and oregano and cook, stirring, until the liquid simmers and begins to thicken slightly, 2 to 3 minutes more. Season to taste with salt and pepper.

As soon as the pasta is done, drain it, toss with the sauce, and serve immediately.

SERVES 4 TO 6

MUSSELS WITH COCONUT CREAM

Thai cooks often complement steamed fresh mussels with the rich sweetness of coconut cream, which you can find in cans in Asian markets or the Asian foods section of well-stocked supermarkets. Use canned or frozen fish broth or, in a pinch, bottled clam juice. When buying any fresh shellfish, make sure to get it from a reputable seafood shop and don't buy it unless it smells absolutely fresh, with the clean scent of the sea and no off odor.

Serve with spaghetti or linguine.

6 tablespoons unsalted butter

6 shallots, sliced thin

2 small fresh hot green chilies such as serranos, halved, stemmed, seeded, and sliced thin

2 cups fish broth or bottled clam juice

1 cup dry white wine

1 lemon, sliced thin

4 dozen small fresh mussels in the shell, scrubbed and bearded

1½ cups heavy cream

1 cup canned coconut cream

¾ pound pasta

Salt

White pepper

6 tablespoons finely chopped fresh cilantro leaves

In a pot large enough to hold all the mussels, melt one-half of the butter over medium heat. Add one-half of the shallots and chilies and sauté 1 to 2 minutes. Add the fish broth, wine, and sliced lemon, bring to a boil, and then reduce the heat to maintain a gentle simmer.

Add the mussels, cover the pan, and steam, turning them over once or twice with a large wooden spoon, until the shells all open, 5 to 7 minutes.

Line a strainer with a double layer of cheesecloth and set it in a large heatproof bowl. Carefully pour the broth through the strainer and set aside. When the mussels are cool enough to handle, shell them and set aside, discarding any that didn't open during cooking.

Bring a large pot of water to a boil.

Return the pan in which you cooked the mussels to medium heat and melt the remaining butter. Add the remaining shallots and chilies and sauté 1 to 2 minutes. Pour the strained broth back into the pan, raise the heat, and boil until reduced by one-half, 7 to 10 minutes. Add the

cream and coconut cream, bring the mixture back to a boil, and simmer briskly until thick and reduced by about one-third, about 10 minutes more.

As soon as you've added the cream and coconut cream, put the pasta in the pot of boiling water and cook until al dente, following the manufacturer's suggested cooking time.

When the pasta is almost done, reduce the heat under the cream mixture and add the shelled mussels. Simmer for 1 minute more to heat through and season the sauce to taste with salt and white pepper.

As soon as the pasta is done, drain it and toss with the mussels and the sauce. Serve immediately in wide bowls and garnish with cilantro.

Serves 4 to 6

Spicy Anchovy Butter with Roasted Garlic

If you are a fan of anchovies in any form, this is the natural next step—and a truly breathtaking experience! There's no need to roast your own garlic: you can find jars of roasted garlic in well-stocked supermarkets, gourmet or Italian delicatessens, and specialty food stores. If you would like to roast garlic, however, separate (but do not peel) the cloves, rub lightly with olive oil, wrap in heavy aluminum foil, and bake at 350ºF until tender, 45 minutes to 1 hour. Let cool, then use your fingers to squeeze each clove of garlic out of its skin.

Serve with thin to medium-width strands or ribbons such as spaghettini, spaghetti, linguine, or tagliatelle.

¾ pound pasta

1 cup (2 sticks) unsalted butter, at room temperature

6 tablespoons anchovy paste

2 cloves roasted garlic or 1 heaping teaspoon pureed roasted garlic

½ tablespoon lemon juice

6 to 12 drops hot red pepper sauce, such as Tabasco

2 tablespoons finely chopped fresh chives

2 tablespoons finely chopped fresh Italian parsley

Grated Parmesan cheese

Bring a large pot of water to a boil. Add the pasta and cook until al dente, following the manufacturer's suggested cooking time.

Meanwhile, put the butter, anchovy paste, roasted garlic, lemon juice, and hot red pepper sauce in a food processor fitted with the metal blade. Process until smooth, stopping once or twice to scrape down the work bowl. Alternatively, simply use a fork to mash the ingredients together in a small bowl.

As soon as the pasta is done, drain it and toss with the butter. Garnish with chopped chives and parsley and serve immediately, passing Parmesan for guests to add to taste.

Serves 4 to 6

Anchovy Pissaladière

The flavors of southern France's ancestral pizza are reproduced in this rapid sauté of onions seasoned with anchovies and Parmesan cheese. Choose the sweetest variety of onions you can find, such as those from Maui, Walla Walla, Vidalia, or Texas.

 *Serve with medium-sized shapes such as wagon wheels or bow ties.*

1¼ cups extra-virgin olive oil

1½ pounds yellow onions, chopped coarse

½ tablespoon sugar

¾ pound pasta

1 2-ounce can anchovy fillets, drained, separated, and chopped coarse

¼ cup finely chopped fresh Italian parsley

Salt

Black pepper

Grated Parmesan cheese

Bring a large pot of water to a boil.

Meanwhile, put the olive oil, onions, and sugar in a large skillet over medium heat. Cook, stirring frequently, until the onions turn translucent and limp, 5 to 7 minutes.

When the water boils, add the pasta and cook until al dente, following the manufacturer's suggested cooking time.

While the pasta is cooking, reduce the heat beneath the skillet to medium-low and continue cooking the onions, stirring frequently, until uniformly golden, 7 to 10 minutes more. Stir in the anchovies and parsley and season to taste with salt and pepper.

As soon as the pasta is done, drain it and toss with the sauce. Serve immediately, passing Parmesan for guests to add to taste.

Serves 4 to 6

SARDINES, TOMATO, AND FRESH DILL

Canned sardines have their devotees, and they will love this simple sauce, which brightens the flavor of the fish with a handful of chopped fresh dill and a touch of tomato.

Serve with spaghetti or other thin to medium-width strands.

¾ pound pasta

6 tablespoons extra-virgin olive oil

1 small onion, chopped fine

1 clove garlic, chopped fine

2 Roma tomatoes, cored and chopped coarse

1 tablespoon double-concentrate tomato paste

1 3¾-ounce can oil-packed sardines, drained

2 tablespoons finely chopped fresh dill

2 tablespoons finely chopped fresh Italian parsley

Salt

Black pepper

¼ cup pine nuts, toasted (see page 7)

Bring a large pot of water to a boil. Add the pasta and cook until al dente, following the manufacturer's suggested cooking time.

While the pasta cooks, prepare the sauce. In a large skillet, heat the olive oil with the onion and garlic over medium-low heat. As soon as the onion begins to turn golden, 3 to 4 minutes, stir in the tomatoes and tomato paste. Sauté about 1 minute more.

Add the sardines, breaking them up with your fingers into coarse pieces, and sauté until heated through, about 1 minute more. Stir in the dill and parsley and season to taste with salt and pepper.

As soon as the pasta is done, drain it and toss with the sauce and the pine nuts. Serve immediately.

SERVES 4 TO 6

Smoked Salmon, Roma Tomatoes, Capers, and Lemon Zest

Utterly simple and fast to prepare, this sauce highlights good-quality smoked salmon with some of its classic companions. Do not use deli-style lox, which is too fatty.

Serve with delicate strands such as angel hair or spaghettini.

¾ pound pasta

3 tablespoons unsalted butter

3 tablespoons extra-virgin olive oil

½ small red onion, chopped fine

1 pound Roma tomatoes, cored and chopped coarse

¼ cup drained capers

2 tablespoons chopped fresh dill or 1 tablespoon dried dill

½ tablespoon sugar

¾ pound thinly sliced smoked salmon, cut into ½-by-1-inch strips

2 tablespoons grated lemon zest

Salt

White pepper

Bring a large pot of water to a boil. Add the pasta and cook until al dente, following the manufacturer's suggested cooking time.

While the pasta cooks, heat the butter, olive oil, and onion in a large frying pan over medium-high heat. As soon as the butter foams and the onion sizzles, add the tomatoes, capers, dill, and sugar and sauté until the tomatoes' juices have thickened but remain fairly fluid, 5 to 7 minutes.

As soon as the pasta is done, drain it, and toss well with the sauce and the smoked salmon and lemon zest. Season to taste with salt and white pepper. Serve immediately.

Serves 4 to 6

GRILLED SALMON WITH TOMATO CREAM AND ARUGULA

Here's a very elegant and easy way to enjoy fresh salmon fillets with pasta. If arugula, the small bitter green also known as rocket, is unavailable, substitute thoroughly washed baby spinach leaves.

Serve with thin to medium-width strands such as spaghettini or spaghetti.

½ cup (1 stick) unsalted butter, cut into pieces

1 pound fresh salmon fillets, skinned and cut into 4 or 6 equal pieces

2 cloves garlic, chopped fine

1 onion, chopped fine

1 28-ounce can crushed tomatoes

2 tablespoons sugar

2 tablespoons double-concentrate tomato paste

½ tablespoon dried basil

½ tablespoon dried oregano

2 bay leaves

¾ pound pasta

Salt

White pepper

½ cup mascarpone or crème fraîche

3 tablespoons finely chopped fresh chives

Preheat the broiler or grill. Bring a large pot of water to a boil.

Meanwhile, melt the butter in a large skillet over medium heat. Put the salmon fillets on a plate and drizzle about one-half of the butter over them, turning the fillets to coat them easily. Set aside.

In the remaining butter, sauté the garlic and onion until they begin to turn translucent, 2 to 3 minutes. Add the tomatoes, sugar, tomato paste, basil, oregano, and bay leaves. Raise the heat to high, bring the sauce to a boil, and then adjust the heat to maintain a brisk simmer and cook, stirring occasionally, until the sauce is thick but still fluid, 10 to 15 minutes.

Partway through the sauce's simmering, add the pasta to the boiling water and cook until al dente, following the manufacturer's suggested cooking time.

At the same time, season the salmon fillets with salt and white pepper and broil or grill until golden brown but still moist inside, 3 to 4 minutes per side, depending on thickness and desired doneness.

A minute or so before the salmon and pasta are done, stir the mascarpone or crème fraîche into the sauce. Season to taste with salt and white pepper and remove the bay leaves.

Drain the pasta, toss, and arrange on individual serving plates or in bowls. Place the salmon on top and garnish with chives.

Serves 4 to 6

SMOKED SALMON WITH VODKA CREAM

Use a good-quality vodka to "spike" the rich sauce of this quick and elegant pasta dish. Most of the alcohol evaporates, leaving the vodka's clean, bracing flavor to complement the richness of both the seafood and the cream. If you're lured by the new rage in flavored vodkas, by all means experiment a little. Lemon and pepper vodkas would work very well here. Also be sure to use good-quality smoked salmon; deli-style lox would be too fatty for this preparation.

 Serve with medium-width strands such as fettuccine. Or try it with bite-sized shapes that hold the cream sauce well, such as radiatore or medium-sized shells.

2 tablespoons unsalted butter

3 shallots, chopped fine

½ cup vodka

4 cups heavy cream

¾ pound pasta

¾ pound thinly sliced smoked salmon, cut into thin, bite-sized strips

Salt

White pepper

2 tablespoons finely chopped fresh Italian parsley

2 tablespoons finely chopped fresh chives

Bring a large pot of water to a boil.

Meanwhile, in a large saucepan or skillet, melt the butter over medium heat. Add the shallots and sauté until they turn translucent, 2 to 3 minutes.

Add the vodka, raise the heat and boil briskly until the vodka reduces by one-half, 4 to 5 minutes. Stir in the cream, bring to a boil, and continue boiling, stirring occasionally, until the sauce is thick and reduced by about one-half, 15 to 20 minutes more.

About halfway through the total reduction time, add the pasta to the boiling water. Cook until al dente, following the manufacturer's suggested cooking time.

Just before the pasta is done, stir the smoked salmon into the sauce and season to taste with salt and white pepper.

When the pasta is done, drain it and toss with the sauce. Garnish with parsley and chives and serve immediately.

 SERVES 4 TO 6

SMOKED SALMON WITH GARLIC-HERB CHEESE

Slivers of smoked salmon go brilliantly well with garlic-herb-flavored, French triple-cream cheeses such as Boursin, easily found in the cheese cases of most well-stocked supermarkets. The combination is ultra-elegant and takes no longer than the time needed to cook the pasta. It is important, though, to have the cheese at room temperature so it will melt with the hot drained pasta. You could warm it very briefly on the lowest setting in your microwave oven, making sure to remove any foil wrapper from the cheese before you put it in the microwave.

Serve with thin to medium-width strands or ribbons such as spaghettini, spaghetti, tagliatelle, or fettuccine.

¾ pound pasta

3 5-ounce packages garlic-herb cream cheese, at room temperature

¾ pound thinly sliced smoked salmon, cut into bite-sized strips

1 tablespoon lemon juice

1 tablespoon grated lemon zest

½ cup finely chopped fresh chives

Black pepper

Bring a large pot of water to a boil. Add the pasta and cook until al dente, following the manufacturer's suggested cooking time.

As soon as the pasta is done, drain it and dot with the cheese. Add the smoked salmon, lemon juice, lemon zest, and chives and toss well, seasoning to taste with pepper. Serve immediately.

SERVES 4 TO 6

SMOKED SALMON, SMOKED TROUT, GOLDEN CAVIAR, AND LEMON-ORANGE BUTTER

Any good delicatessen should have both smoked trout and smoked salmon in stock, along with the relatively inexpensive whitefish roe that is known as golden caviar. Together, these ingredients make a quick pasta dish that looks surpassingly elegant and tastes luxurious.

Serve with angel hair, spaghettini, or spaghetti.

¾ pound pasta

½ cup (1 stick) unsalted butter, cut into pieces

2 shallots, chopped fine

½ tablespoon lemon juice

½ tablespoon orange juice

½ tablespoon grated lemon zest

½ tablespoon grated orange zest

Salt

White pepper

½ pound thinly sliced smoked salmon, cut into ¼-by- 2-inch strips

½ pound smoked trout, boned, skinned, and broken into large flakes

1 tablespoon drained small capers

2 tablespoons golden caviar (whitefish roe)

1 tablespoon finely chopped fresh chives

Bring a large pot of water to a boil. Add the pasta and cook until al dente, following the manufacturer's suggested cooking time.

Meanwhile, in a small skillet, melt the butter over medium heat. Add the shallots and sauté just until they turn translucent, 1 to 2 minutes. Set aside.

As soon as the pasta is done, drain it and transfer to a mixing or serving bowl. Immediately add the butter and shallots and the lemon juice, orange juice, lemon zest, and orange zest and toss well, seasoning to taste with salt and white pepper. Add the smoked salmon, smoked trout, and capers and toss gently but thoroughly.

Immediately transfer the pasta to individual shallow serving bowls or plates, garnish with the golden caviar and chives, and serve.

SERVES 4 TO 6

 TUNA CAPONATA

Italy's sweet-and-sour answer to ratatouille makes a delightful, quick pasta topping when combined with chunks of canned tuna. For the most authentic flavor, use imported tuna canned in olive oil; for a lighter dish, feel free to select water-packed domestic tuna.

Serve with medium-sized shells or other bite-sized shapes.

¾ pound pasta

6 tablespoons extra-virgin olive oil

3 cloves garlic, chopped fine

2 long, slender Asian-style eggplants or 1 small globe eggplant, trimmed, peeled, and cut into ½-inch cubes

1 green bell pepper, stemmed, seeded, and cut into ½-inch pieces

6 Roma tomatoes, cored and chopped coarse

2 tablespoons seedless golden or brown raisins

1 tablespoon drained capers

1 tablespoon sugar

1 tablespoon balsamic or red wine vinegar

1 tablespoon finely chopped fresh parsley

1 tablespoon finely shredded fresh basil leaves

1 teaspoon dried oregano

2 6½-ounce cans tuna, drained and flaked coarsely

Salt

Black pepper

Bring a large pot of water to a boil. Add the pasta and cook until al dente, following the manufacturer's suggested cooking time.

As soon as the pasta starts to cook, heat the olive oil with the garlic in a large skillet over medium-high heat. When the garlic sizzles, add the eggplant and bell pepper and sauté until they just begin to soften and brown, 2 to 3 minutes. Add the tomatoes, raisins, capers, sugar, vinegar, parsley, basil, and oregano and continue sautéing until the eggplant is tender and the tomatoes' juices begin to thicken but are still fairly fluid, 5 to 7 minutes more. About 1 minute before the sauce is done, stir in the tuna to heat it through. Season to taste with salt and pepper.

As soon as the pasta is done, drain it and toss with the sauce. Serve immediately.

SERVES 4 TO 6

Tuna, Olives, Garlic, and Fresh Herbs

If you like olives, you'll love their pungent flavor in this very rapid sauce. For the sake of convenience, you can even buy olives already sliced and the sauce will still taste very good. However, your extra efforts will be rewarded if you track down two or more different kinds of cured olives in a good delicatessen and pit and slice them yourself. A mix of black and green olives looks especially nice.

Serve with pasta shapes such as bow ties, wagon wheels, or fusilli.

¾ pound pasta

¾ cup extra-virgin olive oil

4 cloves garlic, chopped fine

1½ cups mixed pitted and sliced olives, drained well

2 6½-ounce cans oil- or water-packed tuna, drained well and flaked coarse

2 tablespoons finely shredded fresh basil leaves

2 tablespoons finely chopped fresh chives

2 tablespoons finely chopped fresh Italian parsley

½ cup grated Romano cheese, plus extra

Black pepper

Bring a large pot of water to a boil. Add the pasta and cook until al dente, following the manufacturer's suggested cooking time.

A few minutes before the pasta is done, heat the olive oil with the garlic in a large skillet over medium heat. As soon as the garlic sizzles, reduce the heat to low and add the sliced olives. Sauté until the olives are heated through, 1 to 2 minutes more.

As soon as the pasta is done, drain it well and toss with the olive mixture and the tuna, basil, chives, parsley, and ½ cup of Romano. Season to taste with pepper. Serve immediately, passing extra Romano for guests to add to taste.

Serves 4 to 6

TUNA WITH CELERY

There's something delightfully delicate about this simple pasta combination, which you can throw together in a matter of minutes.

Serve with medium-sized shells.

¾ pound pasta

1 cup (2 sticks) unsalted butter

2 teaspoons celery seed

2 celery stalks, cut crosswise into thin slices

2 6½-ounce cans water-packed white albacore tuna, drained and broken into bite-sized flakes

2 tablespoons drained capers

1 tablespoon lemon juice

Salt

White pepper

2 tablespoons finely chopped fresh Italian parsley

Bring a large pot of water to a boil. Add the pasta and cook until al dente, following the manufacturer's suggested cooking time.

A few minutes before the pasta is done, melt the butter in a skillet over medium-low heat. Add the celery seed and cook about 1 minute. Add the sliced celery and sauté about 1 minute more, so that it is warmed but still entirely crisp.

As soon as the pasta is done, toss it with the celery mixture and the tuna, capers, and lemon juice. Season with salt and white pepper to taste. Garnish with parsley and serve immediately.

SERVES 4 TO 6

UNA WITH SPRING PEAS

Try this made-in-an-instant combination when the first fresh pea pods appear in produce stalls.

Serve with delicate to medium-width strands such as angel hair, spaghettini, or spaghetti.

¾ pound pasta

1 cup (2 sticks) unsalted butter, cut into pieces

2 shallots, chopped fine

1½ pounds fresh peas, shelled and parboiled for 2 to 3 minutes

1 6½-ounce can tuna, drained and broken into bite-sized flakes

3 tablespoons lemon juice

2 tablespoons finely chopped fresh chives

1 tablespoon finely chopped fresh mint leaves

Salt

White pepper

Bring a large pot of water to a boil. Add the pasta and cook until al dente, following the manufacturer's suggested cooking time.

Meanwhile, melt the butter in a large skillet over medium-low heat. Add the shallots and sauté about 1 minute. Add the peas and sauté until tender, 2 to 3 minutes more.

As soon as the pasta is done, drain it well and toss with the pea mixture and the tuna, lemon juice, chives, and mint leaves. Season with salt and white pepper to taste. Serve immediately.

SERVES 4 TO 6

Poultry and Meat Sauces

Eggs with Smoked Chicken and Canadian Bacon

Grilled Chicken Alfredo

Grilled Chicken Breasts with Red Bell Pepper–Sun-Dried Tomato Pesto

Ground Chicken Bolognese with Fines Herbes

Ground Chicken and Pine Nut Meatballs with Lemon Butter

Sautéed Chicken with Broccoli, Goat Cheese, Sun-Dried Tomatoes, and Garlic

Roast Chicken with Arugula, Sun-Dried Tomatoes, and Parmesan

Chicken Livers, Prosciutto, and Shiitake Mushrooms with Marsala Cream

Roast Chicken and Chicken Sausage with Tomatoes and Mascarpone

Turkey Breast Piccatta

Mexican Turkey Bolognese

Smoked Turkey with Goat Cheese and Sun-Dried Tomatoes

Turkey Sausage with Artichokes and Tomatoes

Steak with Cherry Tomatoes, Arugula, and Creamy Dressing

Beef and Shiitake Mushroom Bolognese

Chili Sundae

Beef and Sausage Bolognese

Creamy Sausage Bolognese

Chunky Sweet Sausage with Tomato-Chili Cream

Eggs with Sweet Sausage and Brie

Pancetta with Onions, Tomatoes, and Parmesan

Ham with Vegetable Streamers

Grilled White Sausage with Brie and Dijon Cream Sauce

Greek Bolognese with Lamb, Eggplant, Kalamata Olives, and Feta

Grilled Lamb Tenderloin with Pistachio-Mint Pesto

EGGS WITH SMOKED CHICKEN AND CANADIAN BACON

The combination of smoked chicken and lean Canadian bacon gives a wonderfully savory edge to this satisfying breakfast or brunch-style pasta dish. You'll find smoked chicken in well-stocked markets or delicatessens; smoked turkey, more readily available, may be substituted.

Serve with spaghetti or linguine.

¾ pound pasta

8 eggs

¼ cup half-and-half or light cream

¾ cup grated Parmesan cheese

¼ cup (½ stick) unsalted butter, cut into pieces

2 shallots, chopped fine

¾ pound smoked chicken, any skin removed, cut crosswise into thin slices

½ pound Canadian bacon, cut into ¼-inch dice

2 tablespoons finely shredded fresh basil leaves

2 tablespoons finely chopped fresh chives

Black pepper

Bring a large pot of water to a boil. Add the pasta and cook until al dente, following the manufacturer's suggested cooking time.

Meanwhile, in a mixing bowl, lightly beat the eggs. Beat in the half-and-half and the Parmesan. Set aside.

In a large nonstick skillet over medium heat, melt the butter. Add the shallots and sauté about 1 minute. Add the smoked chicken and Canadian bacon and sauté about 1 minute more.

Drain the pasta and add it to the skillet, tossing briefly. Pour the egg mixture over the pasta and cook, stirring and tossing the entire mixture gently, until the eggs form moist curds that cling to the pasta.

Garnish with basil and chives and season to taste with pepper. Serve immediately.

ERVES 4 TO 6

GRILLED CHICKEN ALFREDO

The fabled cheese-and-cream sauce from Alfredo's restaurant in Rome becomes the perfect canvas for strips of quickly grilled chicken breast and red bell pepper.

✄ *Serve with fettuccine or other medium-width ribbons.*

4 boneless, skinless chicken breast halves (about 4 ounces each)

1 cup (2 sticks) unsalted butter, cut into pieces

¾ pound pasta

Salt

Black pepper

1 large red bell pepper, quartered, stemmed, and seeded

1½ cups heavy cream

1½ cups grated Parmesan cheese

2 tablespoons finely shredded fresh basil leaves

2 tablespoons finely chopped fresh chives

Preheat the broiler. Bring a large pot of water to a boil.

Meanwhile, put each chicken breast between two sheets of waxed paper or plastic wrap and roll them with a rolling pin to flatten them to a uniform thickness of about ½ inch. Put them on a large plate or in a shallow dish.

Put the butter in a medium-sized saucepan and melt over medium heat. Pour about one-fourth of the butter over the chicken breasts and turn to coat them evenly; leave the remaining butter in the pan.

Add the pasta to the boiling water and cook until al dente, following the manufacturer's suggested cooking time.

Season the chicken breasts on both sides with salt and black pepper. Place them on a broiler tray and arrange the bell pepper quarters, skin side up, on the tray with them. Broil until the chicken is cooked through and light golden and the peppers are tender, about 5 minutes per side.

While the pasta, chicken, and peppers are cooking, make the Alfredo sauce. Return the pan of melted butter to medium-high heat and add the cream. As soon as the cream begins to simmer, reduce the heat to very low and sprinkle in the Parmesan, stirring continuously until the cheese melts and thickens the sauce.

Drain the pasta and immediately toss with the sauce, and then arrange in individual large shallow serving plates. Cut the chicken breasts crosswise into ½-inch-wide strips and the peppers lengthwise into ¼-inch-wide strips; arrange them on top of each serving. Garnish with basil and chives and serve immediately.

ERVES 4 TO 6

GRILLED CHICKEN BREASTS WITH RED BELL PEPPER– SUN-DRIED TOMATO PESTO

Chicken breasts have become the main course of choice for the health-conscious. And with good reason. Their lightness and satisfying flavor are wonderfully complemented by the bell peppers and sun-dried tomatoes in this attractive, easy presentation. If you like, use chicken "tenders," the thin fillets attached to the breasts that are sometimes removed and sold packaged separately in markets. Cooking the chicken on a charcoal grill or stovetop grill pan will give its surface a crosshatched pattern that adds to the dish's visual interest. To speed up preparation, I call for bottled roasted peppers; you could certainly roast your own if you prefer, following the instructions on page 8.

Serve with medium-width strands or ribbons. Create an especially attractive color combination by using green spinach fettuccine.

¾ cup plus 3 tablespoons extra-virgin olive oil

4½ tablespoons lemon juice

1½ pounds boneless, skinless chicken breast halves or chicken "tenders"

Salt

White pepper

¾ pound pasta

1½ cups bottled roasted red bell peppers, drained

¾ cup drained sun-dried tomatoes

2 cloves garlic

Preheat a stovetop grill pan, charcoal grill, or broiler.

In a mixing bowl, stir together the 3 tablespoons of the olive oil and 3 tablespoons of the lemon juice. Add the chicken breasts and turn them in the mixture to coat well.

Bring a large pot of water to a boil.

Season the chicken breasts all over with salt and white pepper to taste and put them on the grill pan or grill or under the broiler. Grill or broil until cooked through, 4 to 6 minutes per side, depending upon thickness and heat.

½ cup grated Parmesan cheese

2 tablespoons chopped fresh Italian parsley

1 teaspoon crushed red pepper flakes, optional

Partway through the chicken's cooking, add the pasta to the boiling water and cook until al dente, following the manufacturer's suggested cooking time.

Meanwhile, put the remaining ¾ cup olive oil and 1½ tablespoons lemon juice and the roasted peppers, sun-dried tomatoes, garlic, Parmesan, chopped parsley, and, if you like, the red pepper flakes in a food processor fitted with the metal blade. Turning the machine on and off rapidly, pulse the ingredients several times until chopped coarse. Scrape down the work bowl. Then process continuously until the sauce is smooth. Transfer to a mixing bowl.

Just before the pasta is done, if the pesto appears too thick, stir a little of the boiling water from the pasta into the pesto to thin it to a fluid but still fairly thick consistency. Taste the pesto and season to taste with salt and white pepper.

Drain the pasta and immediately toss it with the pesto. Arrange on individual serving plates or in pasta bowls. Cut the chicken breasts crosswise into ¼- to ½-inch-thick slices and place on top of the pasta. Garnish with parsley sprigs.

 ERVES 4 TO 6

GROUND CHICKEN BOLOGNESE WITH FINES HERBES

Though robust in texture, this low-fat variation on a Bolognese sauce has a delicate flavor. You can find ground chicken breast in the meat sections of well-stocked supermarkets, or chop it yourself at home in a food processor fitted with the metal blade. Buy boneless, skinless breasts and cut them into 1-inch chunks before chopping.

Serve with spaghetti or spaghettini.

2 tablespoons extra-virgin olive oil

1 clove garlic, chopped fine

1 shallot, chopped fine

1 pound ground chicken breast

1 28-ounce can crushed tomatoes

2 tablespoons double-concentrate tomato paste

1 tablespoon sugar

1 tablespoon finely chopped fresh Italian parsley

1 tablespoon finely shredded fresh basil leaves

1 teaspoon finely chopped fresh dill

1 teaspoon finely chopped fresh tarragon leaves

1 bay leaf

¾ pound pasta

Salt

Black pepper

Bring a large pot of water to a boil.

As soon as you put the pot over the heat, start cooking the sauce. In a large skillet or saucepan, heat the olive oil over medium heat. Add the garlic and shallot and sauté until the shallot turns translucent, 2 to 3 minutes.

Add the chicken, raise the heat slightly, and sauté, stirring it constantly and breaking it up into fine particles with a wooden spoon, until it has uniformly lost its pink color, 5 to 7 minutes.

Add the tomatoes, tomato paste, sugar, parsley, basil, dill, tarragon, and bay leaf and stir well and scrape the bottom of the pan to dissolve the glaze of meat juices. Bring to a boil and then reduce the heat to maintain a brisk simmer. Cook until the sauce is thick, 15 to 20 minutes, stirring occasionally.

About halfway through the sauce's simmering, add the pasta to the boiling water and cook until al dente, following the manufacturer's suggested cooking time.

Season the sauce with salt and pepper to taste. Remove the bay leaf. As soon as the pasta is done, drain it and toss with the sauce. Serve immediately.

ERVES 4 TO 6

GROUND CHICKEN AND PINE NUT MEATBALLS WITH LEMON BUTTER

One ordinarily thinks of pasta with meatballs as a heavy dish, but this quick poultry version gives the old standard a lighter but nonetheless satisfying touch.

❧ *Serve with spaghetti, linguine, tagliatelle, or fettuccine.*

1 pound ground chicken breast

4 shallots, chopped fine

2 eggs

¾ cup dry bread crumbs

½ cup pine nuts

¼ cup well-drained ricotta cheese

2 tablespoons finely chopped fresh Italian parsley

2 tablespoons finely chopped fresh dill

1 tablespoon finely chopped fresh tarragon leaves

½ teaspoon salt

½ teaspoon white pepper

¾ pound pasta

¾ cup (1½ sticks) unsalted butter, cut into pieces

6 tablespoons lemon juice

¼ cup finely chopped fresh chives

Preheat the broiler and bring a large pot of water to a boil.

Put the chicken, shallots, eggs, bread crumbs, pine nuts, ricotta, parsley, dill, tarragon, salt, and white pepper in a large mixing bowl. With your hands, mix the ingredients thoroughly.

Lightly grease the broiler tray with a little oil or nonstick cooking spray. With a tablespoon and your fingers, form the chicken mixture into meatballs and place them on the broiler tray. Broil them until golden brown all over, turning them once (they'll flatten slightly), about 5 minutes per side.

Meanwhile, put the pasta in the boiling water and cook until al dente, following the manufacturer's suggested cooking time.

When the pasta and meatballs are almost done, melt the butter in a medium-sized saucepan or skillet over medium heat. Stir in the lemon juice and season to taste with salt and white pepper.

As soon as the pasta is done, drain it and toss with the lemon butter. Top with the meatballs, garnish with chives, and serve immediately.

SERVES 4 TO 6

Sautéed Chicken with Broccoli, Goat Cheese, Sun-Dried Tomatoes, and Garlic

This swift sauté of thinly sliced chicken breasts makes a very elegant presentation. Feel free to substitute asparagus for the broccoli and fresh ricotta for the goat cheese, if you like.

Serve with penne, rigatoni, radiatore, bow ties, or other bite-sized tubes or shapes.

1½ cups bite-sized broccoli florets

¾ pound pasta

¾ cup (1½ sticks) unsalted butter, cut into pieces

½ cup extra-virgin olive oil

6 cloves garlic, chopped fine

1 pound boneless, skinless chicken breast halves, trimmed and cut crosswise into ¼-inch-thick slices

Salt

Black pepper

½ cup drained sun-dried tomatoes, cut into thin slivers

½ pound fresh creamy goat cheese, crumbled

2 tablespoons finely shredded fresh basil leaves

2 tablespoons finely chopped fresh Italian parsley

Bring a large pot of water to a boil.

Add the broccoli florets to the water and parboil them until they turn bright green and are tender-crisp, 2 to 3 minutes. Use a wire skimmer or slotted spoon to scoop them from the water. Drain and set aside.

Add the pasta to the boiling water and cook until al dente, following the manufacturer's suggested cooking time.

Meanwhile, heat the butter and olive oil in a large skillet over medium heat. Add the garlic and sauté just until it begins to turn light golden, 1 to 2 minutes. Season the chicken pieces with salt and pepper, add them to the skillet, and sauté, stirring constantly, until the slices begin to turn golden, 3 to 5 minutes more. Add the broccoli and sun-dried tomatoes and sauté about 1 minute more. Season to taste.

As soon as the pasta is done, drain it and toss with the chicken mixture and the goat cheese, basil, and parsley. Serve immediately.

Serves 4 to 6

Roast Chicken with Arugula, Sun-Dried Tomatoes, and Parmesan

The excellent roast chickens found in so many supermarkets and take-out shops today make it easy to prepare a delicious chicken pasta dish like this in less time than it takes for the pasta to cook. You can also make this dish with your own leftover roast chicken. Pull it from the bones and remove the skin.

Serve with medium-width to wide ribbons such as fettuccine or pappardelle or with bite-sized shapes such as radiatore.

¾ pound pasta

½ cup (1 stick) unsalted butter, cut into pieces

¼ cup extra-virgin olive oil

2 shallots, chopped fine

2 cups coarsely shredded roast chicken

½ cup drained sun-dried tomatoes, cut into slivers

1 cup loosely packed arugula leaves

Salt

Black pepper

Grated Parmesan cheese

Bring a large pot of water to a boil. Add the pasta and cook until al dente, following the manufacturer's suggested cooking time.

A few minutes before the pasta is done, melt the butter with the olive oil in a large skillet over medium-low heat. Add the shallots and sauté about 1 minute. Add the chicken and sun-dried tomatoes and sauté just until heated through, 2 to 3 minutes more.

As soon as the pasta is done, drain it and toss with the chicken mixture and the arugula. Season with salt and pepper to taste. Serve immediately, passing Parmesan for guests to add to taste.

ERVES 4 TO 6

CHICKEN LIVERS, PROSCIUTTO, AND SHIITAKE MUSHROOMS WITH MARSALA CREAM

The many people who love chicken livers will adore this luxurious sauce. You'll find prosciutto in Italian delicatessens and in the deli counters of well-stocked supermarkets. Regular mushrooms may be substituted for the shiitakes.

❧ *Serve with medium-width strands such as fettuccine, with medium-sized shells, or with shapes that will hold the sauce well such as radiatore.*

¼ cup (½ stick) unsalted butter, cut into pieces

4 shallots, chopped fine

2 ounces thinly sliced prosciutto, cut into ¼-by-1-inch strips

1 pound chicken livers, trimmed and cut into ½-inch pieces

¾ pound shiitake mushrooms, stems trimmed and discarded, caps cut into ¼-inch-thick slices

¾ pound pasta

Bring a large pot of water to a boil.

Meanwhile, melt half of the butter in a large skillet over medium heat. Add the shallots and prosciutto and sauté just until the shallots start to turn translucent, 1 to 2 minutes. Add the chicken livers, raise the heat slightly, and sauté until they are lightly browned, about 3 minutes more. Remove the chicken liver mixture from the skillet and set aside.

In the same skillet, melt the remaining butter over medium-high heat. Add the mushrooms and sauté until their edges begin to turn golden, 3 to 5 minutes. Remove them from the skillet, adding them to the chicken liver mixture.

Add the pasta to the boiling water and cook until al dente, following the manufacturer's suggested cooking time.

½ cup chicken broth

½ cup marsala wine

½ teaspoon dried tarragon

1 cup heavy cream

Salt

White pepper

2 tablespoons finely chopped fresh
    Italian parsley

2 tablespoons finely chopped fresh
    chives

Grated Parmesan cheese

As soon as the pasta starts cooking, add the chicken broth and marsala to the skillet and cook over medium-high heat, stirring and scraping with a wooden spoon to dissolve the glaze of juices on the bottom. Crumble in the tarragon and boil for 1 to 2 minutes, until the liquids reduce slightly. Stir in the cream and simmer briskly until a thick sauce forms, 5 to 7 minutes more, returning the chicken liver and mushroom mixture to the skillet for the last 2 minutes or so to heat through. Season to taste with salt and white pepper.

As soon as the pasta is done, drain it and toss with the sauce and the parsley and chives. Serve immediately, passing the Parmesan for guests to add to taste.

 Serves 4 to 6

ROAST CHICKEN AND CHICKEN SAUSAGE WITH TOMATOES AND MASCARPONE

Use a store-bought roast chicken or your own leftovers for this quick dish. It also features the fresh chicken sausages you'll find in the meat department of well-stocked supermarkets and butcher shops today; select a spicy one, if you like, or one of the popular varieties seasoned with sun-dried tomatoes. In place of mascarpone, the popular lightly soured cream cheese found in Italian delicatessens and upscale markets, you may use French crème fraîche or equal parts of heavy cream and sour cream.

Serve with medium-width to wide ribbons such as fettuccine or pappardelle or with bite-sized shapes such as farfalle or radiatore.

¾ pound pasta

¼ cup extra-virgin olive oil

2 shallots, chopped fine

2 fresh chicken sausages (about ½ pound total), casings slit and removed

¾ pound Roma tomatoes, cored and chopped coarse

1 teaspoon sugar

1 cup coarsely shredded roast chicken

¼ cup finely shredded fresh basil leaves

Salt

Black pepper

½ cup mascarpone, at room temperature

Bring a large pot of water to a boil. Add the pasta and cook until al dente, following the manufacturer's suggested cooking time.

Meanwhile, heat the olive oil in a large skillet over medium heat. Add the shallots and sauté about 1 minute. Add the chicken sausage and sauté, breaking it up into small, bite-sized pieces, until it has uniformly lost its pink color and is lightly browned, 3 to 5 minutes.

Add the tomatoes and sugar and sauté until the tomatoes' juices have begun to thicken, 2 to 3 minutes more. Add the shredded chicken and basil and sauté until heated through, 1 to 2 minutes more. Season to taste with salt and pepper.

As soon as the pasta is done, drain it and toss with the chicken mixture and the mascarpone. Serve immediately.

 ERVES 4 TO 6

TURKEY BREAST PICCATA

This quick pasta topping becomes especially easy to make thanks to the ready-to-cook slices of fresh, raw turkey breast now sold packaged in so many supermarkets. You can also make it with boneless, skinless chicken breast halves that you've flattened to a uniform thickness between two sheets of waxed paper or plastic wrap, or with thin cutlets of veal.

Serve with linguine, tagliatelle, fettuccine, or other medium-width strands or ribbons.

¾ pound pasta

½ pound (2 sticks) unsalted butter, cut into pieces

¼ cup extra-virgin olive oil

2 cloves garlic, chopped fine

1½ pounds uncooked turkey breast slices

Salt

White pepper

6 tablespoons lemon juice

2 tablespoons grated lemon zest

4 tablespoons drained capers

2 tablespoons finely chopped fresh Italian parsley

Bring a large pot of water to a boil. Add the pasta and cook until al dente, following the manufacturer's suggested cooking time.

As soon as the pasta starts cooking, put about 4 tablespoons (½ stick) of the butter and the olive oil and garlic in one or two frying pans large enough to hold the turkey slices in a single layer without crowding. Place the pan or pans over medium-high heat. When the butter begins to foam, season the turkey slices on both sides with salt and white pepper and cook them until lightly golden, 3 to 4 minutes per side. Remove them from the pan and keep warm.

Reduce the heat to low, add the remaining butter and the lemon juice and lemon zest to the pan and stir continuously until the butter melts, scraping the bottom of the pan to dissolve the glaze of meat juices. Stir in the capers, taste the sauce, and add a little more salt and white pepper to taste if necessary.

As soon as the pasta is done, toss it with the sauce. Cut the turkey slices crosswise into ¼- to ½-inch-wide strips and place them on top of the pasta. Garnish with parsley and serve immediately.

SERVES 4 TO 6

Mexican Turkey Bolognese

Ground turkey has become a popular, healthy alternative to ground beef. Here, it figures in a Bolognese-style sauce with a lively south-of-the-border flourish. The jalapeño pepper will not make this sauce unbearably spicy if you make sure to remove all its seeds and white veins. When handling the jalapeño pepper, take care not to let its oils come in contact with your eyes, any cuts or abrasions, or other sensitive areas. To that end, wear kitchen gloves or at least be sure to wash your hands thoroughly with soap and warm water when you're through.

Serve with medium-width strands such as spaghetti or linguine or with bite-sized shapes such as wagon wheels or radiatore.

¼ cup extra-virgin olive oil

2 cloves garlic, chopped fine

1 onion, chopped fine

1 jalapeño pepper, halved, stemmed, seeded, white veins removed and discarded, chopped fine

1 red or green bell pepper, halved, stemmed, and seeded, cut into ½-inch dice

1 pound ground turkey

1 28-ounce can crushed tomatoes

2 tablespoons double-concentrate tomato paste

1 tablespoon dried oregano

½ tablespoon sugar

2 bay leaves

Bring a large pot of water to a boil.

As soon as you put the pot over the heat, start cooking the sauce. In a large skillet or saucepan, heat the olive oil over medium heat. Add the garlic, onion, jalapeño pepper, and bell pepper dice and sauté until the onion turns translucent, 2 to 3 minutes.

Add the turkey, raise the heat slightly, and sauté, stirring constantly and breaking it up into fine particles with a wooden spoon, until it has uniformly lost its pink color, 5 to 7 minutes. Carefully pour off any fat.

Return the skillet or pan to the heat. Add the tomatoes, tomato paste, oregano, sugar, and bay leaves and stir well and scrape the bottom of the pan to dissolve the glaze of meat juices. Bring to a boil, reduce the heat to maintain a brisk simmer, and cook until the sauce is thick, 15 to 20 minutes, stirring occasionally.

¾ pound pasta

1 cup drained canned niblet corn

¼ cup coarsely chopped fresh
    cilantro leaves

Salt

Black pepper

About halfway through the sauce's simmering, add the pasta to the boiling water and cook until al dente, following the manufacturer's suggested cooking time.

About 1 minute before the pasta is done, add the corn and cilantro to the sauce and season to taste with salt and black pepper; remove the bay leaves. As soon as the pasta is done, drain it and toss with the sauce. Serve immediately.

Serves 4 to 6

SMOKED TURKEY WITH GOAT CHEESE AND SUN-DRIED TOMATOES

The rich, sweet-edged flavor of smoked turkey contrasts enticingly with the luscious tang of creamy goat cheese and the intensity of sun-dried tomatoes.

Serve with medium-width to wide ribbons such as fettuccine or pappardelle.

¾ pound pasta

2 tablespoons unsalted butter

2 shallots, chopped fine

1 cup heavy cream

¼ pound fresh creamy goat cheese, cut into chunks

1 pound smoked turkey, sliced thin and cut crosswise into ¼-inch-wide strips

½ cup drained sun-dried tomatoes, cut into thin slivers

Salt

Black pepper

¼ cup pine nuts, toasted (see page 7)

2 tablespoons finely shredded fresh basil leaves

2 tablespoons finely chopped fresh chives

Bring a large pot of water to a boil. Add the pasta and cook until al dente, following the manufacturer's suggested cooking time.

Meanwhile, in a medium-sized saucepan or skillet, melt the butter over medium heat. Add the shallots and sauté about 1 minute. Add the cream and bring it to a boil. Add the goat cheese, reduce the heat and simmer, stirring continuously, until the goat cheese melts and thickens the sauce.

Stir in the smoked turkey and sun-dried tomatoes and simmer until heated through, 1 to 2 minutes more. Season to taste with salt and pepper.

As soon as the pasta is done, drain it and toss with the sauce and with the pine nuts, basil, and chives. Serve immediately.

 SERVES 4 TO 6

TURKEY SAUSAGE
WITH ARTICHOKES AND TOMATOES

A rapid sauté acquires the body and flavor of a robust, long-simmered sauce in this very flavorful pasta dish. Most markets today carry fresh turkey sausages; look for the spicy Italian style, though any well-seasoned type will do.

Serve with medium-width ribbons such as fettuccine or tagliatelle or with bite-sized shapes such as radiatore or wagon wheels.

2 tablespoons extra-virgin olive oil

2 cloves garlic, chopped fine

1 pound Italian-style fresh turkey sausages, casings slit and removed

1 pound Roma tomatoes, cored and chopped coarse

1 cup marinated artichoke hearts, drained, any whole hearts cut into bite-sized quarters or halves

2 tablespoons finely shredded fresh basil leaves

½ tablespoon sugar

¾ pound pasta

Salt

Black pepper

Bring a large pot of water to a boil.

Heat the olive oil and garlic in a large frying pan over medium-high heat. As soon as the garlic sizzles, add the sausage and sauté, stirring it constantly and breaking it up into coarse chunks with a wooden spoon, until it has uniformly lost its pink color, 5 to 7 minutes.

Pour off excess fat from the skillet and return the skillet to the heat. Add the tomatoes, artichoke hearts, basil, and sugar. Sauté until the ingredients are heated through and the tomatoes' juices have thickened but remain fairly fluid, 5 to 7 minutes.

As soon as you add the tomatoes and other ingredients, put the pasta in the boiling water and cook until al dente, following the manufacturer's suggested cooking time.

Season the sauce to taste with salt and pepper and, if necessary, cover to keep warm.

As soon as the pasta is done, drain it and toss well with the sauce. Serve immediately.

 ERVES 4 TO 6

STEAK WITH CHERRY TOMATOES, ARUGULA, AND CREAMY DRESSING

Think of this as a sort of warm pasta salad, featuring some of the favorite steak house accompaniments for a good cut of beef.

Serve with medium-sized pasta shapes such as wagon wheels, radiatore, or bow ties.

¾ pound pasta

1½ pounds beef sirloin, filet, or tenderloin steak, completely trimmed of fat and gristle

Salt

Black pepper

¼ cup cream

1 cup creamy blue-cheese or ranch-style dressing

6 Roma tomatoes, cored and chopped coarse

1 cup packed arugula leaves

½ red onion, chopped fine

4 tablespoons finely chopped fresh chives

Preheat the broiler.

Bring a large pot of water to a boil. Add the pasta and cook until al dente, following the manufacturer's suggested cooking time.

As soon as the pasta starts cooking, season the steak generously to taste on both sides with salt and pepper. Broil it about 5 minutes per side for medium-rare.

While the steak and pasta cook, heat the cream in a small saucepan over medium heat. Add the dressing, reduce the heat to low, and cook just until it turns lukewarm.

As soon as the pasta is done, toss it with the warm dressing and the tomatoes, arugula leaves, and red onion and divide it among individual serving plates or bowls. The moment the steak is done, cut it crosswise on the diagonal into ¼-inch-thick slices and drape them over the pasta. Garnish with chives and serve immediately.

ERVES 4 TO 6

Beef and Shiitake Mushroom Bolognese

This recipe lowers the fat and cholesterol of Bolognese while still offering the robust flavor of good beef by substituting meaty-tasting shiitake mushrooms for one-half of the meat.

Serve with spaghetti or any other basic pasta.

¼ cup extra-virgin olive oil

4 cloves garlic, chopped fine

1 large onion, chopped fine

½ pound ground beef

¾ pound fresh shiitake mushrooms, stems trimmed and discarded, caps chopped coarse

1 28-ounce can crushed tomatoes

2 tablespoons double-concentrate tomato paste

1 tablespoon dried oregano

1 tablespoon dried basil

½ tablespoon sugar

2 bay leaves

¾ pound pasta

Salt

Black pepper

Bring a large pot of water to a boil.

As soon as you put the pot over the heat, start cooking the sauce. In a large skillet or saucepan, heat the olive oil over medium heat. Add the garlic and onion and sauté until the onion turns translucent, 2 to 3 minutes.

Add the beef and shiitake mushrooms, raise the heat slightly, and sauté, stirring constantly and breaking up the meat into fine particles with a wooden spoon, until the beef has uniformly lost its pink color, 5 to 7 minutes. Carefully pour off any fat.

Return the skillet or pan to the heat. Add the tomatoes, tomato paste, oregano, basil, sugar, and bay leaves and stir well. Bring to a boil, reduce the heat to maintain a brisk simmer, and cook until the sauce is thick, 15 to 20 minutes.

About halfway through the sauce's simmering, add the pasta to the boiling water and cook until al dente, following the manufacturer's suggested cooking time.

Before the pasta is done, taste the sauce and season with salt and pepper to taste; remove the bay leaves. As soon as the pasta is done, drain it and toss with the sauce. Serve immediately.

 erves 4 to 6

CHILI SUNDAE

One of my favorite childhood lunch counter meals was the dish known as a "chili sundae," in which spaghetti, a thick meat chili, cheese, and onions visually mimic the soda fountain treat. The sauce featured in this recipe has the consistency of a thick, Italian-style meat sauce, with all the flavor of the kind of classic chili you find ladled over a really good chili dog.

Of course, you can serve it with spaghetti or other medium-width strands or ribbons. It's also fun with wagon wheels or bow ties.

¼ cup vegetable oil

2 cloves garlic, chopped very fine

1 yellow onion, chopped very fine

4 tablespoons pure red chili powder

½ tablespoon sugar

1 teaspoon ground cumin

1½ pounds ground beef, pork, or both

1½ cups beef or chicken broth

¼ cup yellow cornmeal

3 tablespoons tomato paste

1 teaspoon dried oregano

1 bay leaf

¾ pound pasta

Salt

Black pepper

¼ pound cheddar cheese, shredded

½ small red onion, chopped fine

Bring a large pot of water to a boil.

Meanwhile, in a medium-sized saucepan, heat the vegetable oil over medium heat. Add the garlic and onion and sauté until translucent, 3 to 4 minutes. Stir in the pure red chili powder, sugar, and cumin and sauté about 1 minute more. Add the meat and sauté, stirring it constantly and breaking it up into very small particles with a wooden spoon, until evenly browned, about 5 minutes more.

Stir in the broth, cornmeal, tomato paste, oregano, and bay leaf, reduce the heat to medium-low, and simmer, stirring occasionally, until the sauce is very thick but still slightly fluid, 12 to 15 minutes more.

While the sauce is simmering, add the pasta to the boiling water and cook until al dente, following the manufacturer's suggested cooking time.

When the sauce is ready, season it to taste with salt and pepper and remove the bay leaf. As soon as the pasta is done, drain it and place it in individual shallow serving bowls or a large serving bowl and top with the meat sauce. Garnish with cheddar cheese and red onion and serve immediately.

SERVES 4 TO 6

BEEF AND SAUSAGE BOLOGNESE

Adding ground Italian sausage—your choice of spicy or sweet—to the beef in a traditional Bolognese sauce adds another dimension of rich savor.

Serve this robust sauce with medium-width strands or ribbons such as spaghetti, linguine, or fettuccine.

¼ cup extra-virgin olive oil

3 cloves garlic, chopped fine

1 large onion, chopped fine

½ pound lean ground beef

½ pound fresh Italian pork sausages, casings slit and removed

½ cup dry red wine

1 28-ounce can crushed tomatoes

2 tablespoons double-concentrate tomato paste

2 tablespoons finely chopped fresh Italian parsley

1 tablespoon dried oregano

½ tablespoon dried basil

½ tablespoon sugar

2 bay leaves

¾ pound pasta

Salt

Black pepper

Bring a large pot of water to a boil.

As soon as you put the pot over the heat, start cooking the sauce. In a large skillet or saucepan, heat the olive oil over medium heat. Add the garlic and onion and sauté until the onion turns translucent, 2 to 3 minutes.

Add the beef and sausage, raise the heat slightly, and sauté, stirring the meat constantly and breaking it up into fine particles with a wooden spoon, until it has uniformly lost its pink color, 5 to 7 minutes. Carefully pour off any fat.

Return the skillet or pan to the heat, add the wine, and stir and scrape the bottom of the skillet with the wooden spoon to dissolve the glaze of meat juices. Add the tomatoes, tomato paste, parsley, oregano, basil, sugar, and bay leaves and stir well. Bring to a boil, reduce the heat to maintain a brisk simmer, and cook until the sauce is thick, 15 to 20 minutes.

About halfway through the sauce's simmering, add the pasta to the boiling water and cook until al dente, following the manufacturer's suggested cooking time.

Before the pasta is done, taste the sauce and season with salt and pepper to taste; remove the bay leaves. As soon as the pasta is done, drain it and toss with the sauce. Serve immediately.

ERVES 4 TO 6

CREAMY SAUSAGE BOLOGNESE

Spicy Italian-style sausage adds a wonderfully hearty dimension to a classic Bolognese-style sauce, which then gains richness and surprising elegance from a splash of cream. If you like, use fresh Italian turkey sausages, widely available in markets today, in place of pork sausage. Of course, you may also use sweet, fennel-scented Italian sausage instead of spicy.

Serve with medium-width strands or ribbons such as spaghetti, linguine, or fettuccine or with medium-sized shells.

¼ cup unsalted butter

2 cloves garlic, chopped fine

1 small onion, chopped fine

1 carrot, chopped fine

1 pound spicy Italian pork sausages, casings slit and removed

1 28-ounce can crushed tomatoes

1 tablespoon double-concentrate tomato paste

1 tablespoon dried oregano

1 tablespoon dried basil

½ tablespoon sugar

1 bay leaf

¾ pound pasta

½ cup heavy cream

Salt

Black pepper

In a large skillet or saucepan, melt the butter over medium-low heat. Add the garlic, onion, and carrot and sauté until the onion turns translucent, 2 to 3 minutes.

Raise the heat slightly, crumble in the sausage, and sauté, stirring it constantly and breaking up the meat with a wooden spoon, until it has uniformly lost its pink color and left a brown glaze on the bottom of the pan, about 10 minutes.

Add the tomatoes, tomato paste, oregano, basil, sugar, and bay leaf. Stir and scrape the bottom of the pan with the wooden spoon to dissolve the glaze of meat juices. Cook the sauce at a gentle simmer until thick, 15 to 20 minutes.

Meanwhile, bring a large pot of water to a boil. Add the pasta and cook until al dente, following the manufacturer's suggested cooking time.

Just before the pasta is done, remove the bay leaf from the sauce and stir in the cream. Season to taste with salt and pepper.

When the pasta is done, drain it and toss with the sauce. Serve immediately.

SERVES 4 TO 6

CHUNKY SWEET SAUSAGE WITH TOMATO-CHILI CREAM

You can find all kinds of fresh, sweet (that is, not spicy) Italian-style sausage in Italian delicatessens and good-quality markets today. I especially like to make this dish with turkey or chicken sausage, but traditional Italian pork sausage tastes just as good. By "bottled chili sauce," called for in the ingredients, I do not mean superhot red pepper sauces typified by the Tabasco brand; rather, I mean the old-fashioned, thick, mild, and slightly sweet-tasting tomato-based bottled chili sauces such as those made by Heinz and found in the condiments sections of most markets.

Serve with medium-width strands or ribbons or medium-sized shapes—spaghetti, fettuccine, or bow ties, for example.

2 tablespoons unsalted butter

2 tablespoons vegetable oil

2 cloves garlic, chopped fine

½ onion, chopped fine

1½ pounds fresh sweet Italian-style sausages, casings slit and removed

1½ cups heavy cream

¾ pound pasta

1 cup bottled tomato-based chili sauce

Bring a large pot of water to a boil.

Meanwhile, melt the butter with the vegetable oil in a large skillet over medium heat. Add the garlic and onion and sauté until the onion is translucent, 2 to 3 minutes. Add the sausage, breaking it with your fingers into bite-sized chunks about 1 inch in diameter as you drop it in. Sauté, stirring frequently, until the sausage chunks are evenly browned, 5 to 7 minutes. Remove the sausage chunks, onion, and garlic to a dish, set them aside, and drain excess fat from the skillet.

Put the cream in the skillet over medium heat and boil it gently until it reduces by about one-third, 7 to 10 minutes.

As soon as the cream starts boiling, put the pasta in the pot of boiling water and cook until al dente, following the manufacturer's suggested cooking time.

When the cream is thickened, stir in the chili sauce and the reserved sausage, onion, and garlic and cook until heated through, 1 to 2 minutes more.

As soon as the pasta is done, drain it. Add the sauce and toss well. Serve immediately.

SERVES 4 TO 6

Eggs with Sweet Sausage and Brie

This breakfast-style pasta features fresh, sweet Italian sausage, the kind that contains whole fennel seeds. You'll find it in most well-stocked supermarkets, as well as in Italian delicatessens. While the sausages are commonly made from pork or beef, you can also find turkey versions nowadays.

Serve with spaghetti or linguine.

¾ pound pasta

8 eggs

¼ cup half-and-half or light cream

½ cup grated Parmesan cheese

1 pound fresh sweet Italian sausages, casings slit and removed, meat broken up into small bite-sized pieces

¼ cup (½ stick) unsalted butter, cut into pieces

2 cloves garlic, chopped fine

½ pound ripe Brie, rind cut off, at room temperature

2 tablespoons finely chopped fresh chives

2 tablespoons finely chopped fresh Italian parsley

Black pepper

Bring a large pot of water to a boil. Add the pasta and cook until al dente, following the manufacturer's suggested cooking time.

Meanwhile, in a mixing bowl, lightly beat the eggs. Beat in the half-and-half and the Parmesan. Set aside.

In a large nonstick skillet over medium heat, sauté the sausage until lightly browned, 3 to 4 minutes. Carefully pour off the fat and set the sausage pieces aside.

Melt the butter in the skillet over medium-low heat. Add the garlic and sauté for about 1 minute. Drain the pasta and add it to the skillet, tossing briefly with the butter and garlic. Pour the egg mixture over the pasta and cook, stirring and tossing the entire mixture gently, until the egg begins to thicken and coat the pasta. Add the sausage pieces and, with your fingertips, drop in small clumps of the Brie. Continue cooking until the Brie melts and the eggs form moist curds that cling to the pasta.

Garnish with chives and parsley and season to taste with pepper. Serve immediately.

Serves 4 to 6

PANCETTA WITH ONIONS, TOMATOES, AND PARMESAN

This rapid sauce relies on the salty-sweet flavor of pancetta, the Italian bacon usually sold in slices cut from a large, rolled slab in Italian delicatessens. You can substitute any other good-quality bacon.

Serve with spaghettini, spaghetti, linguine, tagliatelle, or other thin to medium-width strands or ribbons.

¾ pound pasta

¼ cup extra-virgin olive oil

¾ pound pancetta, sliced thin and cut into ¼- to ½-inch pieces

2 onions, chopped coarse

2 cloves garlic, chopped coarse

1 pound Roma tomatoes, cored and chopped coarse

½ tablespoon sugar

2 teaspoons dried oregano

Salt

Black pepper

2 tablespoons finely shredded fresh basil leaves

2 tablespoons finely chopped fresh Italian parsley

Bring a large pot of water to a boil. Add the pasta and cook until al dente, following the manufacturer's suggested cooking time.

As soon as the pasta starts cooking, heat the olive oil in a large skillet over medium heat. Add the pancetta, onions, and garlic and sauté 2 to 3 minutes, until the onions begin to turn translucent and the pancetta has uniformly lost its raw color.

Add the tomatoes, sugar, and oregano to the skillet, raise the heat and sauté just until the tomatoes' juices begin to thicken, 3 to 4 minutes more. Season to taste with salt and pepper.

As soon as the pasta is done, drain it and toss with the pancetta mixture and the basil and parsley. Serve immediately.

SERVES 4 TO 6

HAM WITH VEGETABLE STREAMERS

You'll be especially thankful for this speedy pasta dish when you've got leftover ham in the refrigerator. But don't wait until then to make it. Buy the best-quality cooked smoked ham you can find. Use your food processor to shred the vegetables or shred them by hand on the medium-sized holes of a handheld grater/shredder.

❧ *Serve with spaghetti, fettuccine, or other medium-width strands or ribbons or with bite-sized shapes or tubes such as bow ties, radiatore, or rigatoni.*

¾ pound pasta

½ cup (1 stick) unsalted butter, cut into pieces

¼ cup extra-virgin olive oil

4 shallots, chopped fine

1 medium-sized zucchini, cut into long shreds

1 medium-sized yellow summer squash, cut into long shreds

1 medium-sized carrot, cut into long shreds

1 red bell pepper, quartered, stemmed, seeded, quarters cut crosswise into very thin strips

2 cups packed coarsely shredded ham (about 1 pound)

Salt

Black pepper

2 tablespoons finely shredded fresh basil leaves

2 tablespoons finely chopped fresh Italian parsley

Grated Parmesan cheese

Bring a large pot of water to a boil. Add the pasta and cook until al dente, following the manufacturer's suggested cooking time.

About halfway through the pasta's cooking time, heat the butter and olive oil in a large skillet over medium heat. Add the shallots and sauté about 1 minute. Add the zucchini, summer squash, carrot, and bell pepper and sauté, stirring, until the vegetables are barely tender-crisp, 1 to 2 minutes more. Add the ham and sauté until heated through, about 1 minute more. Season to taste with salt and black pepper.

As soon as the pasta is done, drain it and toss with the vegetable mixture and the basil and parsley. Serve immediately, passing Parmesan for guests to add to taste.

*S*ERVES 4 TO 6

GRILLED WHITE SAUSAGE WITH BRIE AND DIJON CREAM SAUCE

Robust yet ultra-elegant, this pasta topping is richly satisfying. Well-stocked supermarkets and butcher shops will sell some variation on weisswurst, *the ivory-colored veal or pork sausage. Often, you'll find it vacuum-packed and precooked, requiring just heating and grilling; the cooking instructions given here will not vary, however.*

Serve with medium-width ribbons such as fettuccine.

4 *weisswurst* sausages (about 1 pound)

¾ pound pasta

2 cups heavy cream

½ pound ripe Brie, rind cut off, at room temperature

½ cup grated Parmesan cheese

2 tablespoons grainy Dijon-style mustard

Salt

White pepper

3 tablespoons finely chopped fresh chives

Preheat the broiler or grill. Meanwhile, use a fork to puncture the sausages in a few places. Put them in a large pot of water and bring to a boil.

As soon as the water boils, use a skimmer or slotted spoon to remove the sausages. Add the pasta to the boiling water and cook until al dente, following the manufacturer's suggested cooking time.

As soon as the pasta starts cooking, put the cream in a saucepan and bring to a boil over medium-high heat. At the same time, put the sausages under the broiler or on the grill and cook until golden brown, 3 to 4 minutes per side.

When the cream boils, reduce the heat slightly and add the Brie, stirring until it begins to melt. Stir in the Parmesan and then the mustard, continuing to cook and stir until the sauce thickens, 3 to 4 minutes. Season to taste with salt and white pepper.

As soon as the pasta is done, drain it and toss with the sauce. Arrange the pasta in individual serving bowls. Cut the sausages on the diagonal into ½-inch-thick slices and arrange them on top of the pasta, garnishing with chives. Serve immediately.

SERVES 4 TO 6

GREEK BOLOGNESE WITH LAMB, EGGPLANT, KALAMATA OLIVES, AND FETA

To the surprise of just about everyone but those who know Greece well, pasta is very popular there. This recipe recognizes that fact with a sauce that looks like a classic Bolognese meat sauce but whose formula is varied with traditional Greek ingredients and seasonings.

✦ *Serve with spaghetti or linguine or with bite-sized tubes or shapes such as penne, rigatoni, or bow ties.*

¼ cup extra-virgin olive oil

2 cloves garlic, chopped fine

1 onion, chopped fine

1 pound lean ground lamb

¼ teaspoon ground cinnamon

Pinch of ground nutmeg

2 long, slender Asian-style eggplants or 1 small globe eggplant, trimmed, peeled, and cut into ½-inch dice

1 28-ounce can crushed tomatoes

2 tablespoons double-concentrate tomato paste

1 tablespoon dried oregano

½ tablespoon dried basil

½ tablespoon sugar

2 bay leaves

Bring a large pot of water to a boil.

As soon as you put the pot over the heat, start cooking the sauce. In a large skillet or saucepan, heat the olive oil over medium heat. Add the garlic and onion and sauté until the onion turns translucent, 2 to 3 minutes.

Add the lamb, raise the heat slightly, and sauté, stirring it constantly and breaking it up into fine particles with a wooden spoon, until it has uniformly lost its pink color, 5 to 7 minutes. Carefully pour off any fat.

Return the skillet or pan to the heat and sprinkle in the cinnamon and nutmeg, stirring briefly. Add the eggplant, tomatoes, tomato paste, oregano, basil, sugar, and bay leaves and stir well, scraping the bottom of the pan to dissolve the glaze of meat juices. Bring to a boil, reduce the heat to maintain a brisk simmer, and cook until the sauce is thick, 15 to 20 minutes, stirring occasionally.

¾ pound pasta

¾ cup pitted and chopped Kalamata
    olives or other brine-cured black olives

Salt

Black pepper

6 ounces feta cheese, crumbled

About halfway through the sauce's simmering, add the pasta to the boiling water and cook until al dente, following the manufacturer's suggested cooking time.

About 1 minute before the pasta is done, add the olives to the sauce and season to taste with salt and pepper; remove the bay leaves. As soon as the pasta is done, drain it and toss with the sauce and the crumbled feta. Serve immediately.

ERVES 4 TO 6

GRILLED LAMB TENDERLOIN WITH PISTACHIO-MINT PESTO

The bright-green pesto sauce is also delightful on its own, but its flavors complement quickly cooked lamb tenderloin especially well. Well-stocked supermarkets or specialty food stores will sell shelled roasted pistachios.

Serve over medium-width ribbons such as tagliatelle or fettuccine.

1½ cups plus 2 tablespoons extra-virgin olive oil

2 tablespoons lemon juice

1½ pounds lamb tenderloin, trimmed well

¾ pound pasta

Salt

Black pepper

2 cups packed fresh Italian parsley

1 cup packed fresh mint leaves

¾ cup shelled roasted pistachio nuts

1 cup grated Parmesan cheese

3 cloves garlic, peeled

In a shallow bowl, stir together the 2 tablespoons of olive oil and the lemon juice and turn the lamb tenderloin in it to coat it well. Leave to marinate at room temperature while you preheat a grill or broiler and bring a large pot of water to a boil.

Add the pasta to the water and cook until al dente, following the manufacturer's suggested cooking time.

At the same time, season the tenderloin all over with salt and pepper and grill or broil it to taste, 3 to 4 minutes per side for medium-rare. Discard the marinade.

While the lamb and pasta are cooking, put the remaining olive oil, parsley, mint, pistachios, Parmesan, and garlic in a food processor fitted with the metal blade. Turning the machine on and off rapidly, pulse the ingredients several times until chopped coarse. Scrape down the work bowl. Then process continuously until the sauce is smooth. If the pesto seems too thick, pulse in a little boiling water from the pasta.

As soon as the pasta is done, drain it, toss with the pesto, and arrange in beds in individual shallow serving bowls or on plates. Cut the lamb tenderloin crosswise into ¼- to ½-inch-thick slices and arrange them on top. Serve immediately.

SERVES 4 TO 6

Vegetable Sauces

Marinara with Fennel and Fresh Herbs*

Roma Tomatoes with Pesto and Fresh Mozzarella**

Fresh Tomatoes, Mint, and Ricotta**

Tomato-Onion Sauce with Prosciutto and Mozzarella

Spicy Tomato with Fresh Goat Cheese**

Broiled Eggplant, Fresh Tomatoes, and Basil*

Curried Mushroom and Tomato**

Herbed Button Mushroom Marinara**

Wild Mushroom and Leek Cream with Mascarpone**

Artichoke and Tomato Sauté*

Sauté of Fava Beans, Peas, and Artichokes with Fresh Ricotta**

Asparagus with Browned Butter, Lemon Zest, and Parmesan Shavings**

Asparagus, Fresh Tomatoes, and Cream**

Mushroom, Bacon, and Pine Nut Sauté

* This recipe is vegan; that is, it contains no animal products whatsoever.
** This recipe uses dairy or eggs but no other animal products.

*Shiitake Mushroom and Garlic Sauté***

*Asparagus, Shiitake Mushrooms, Sun-Dried Tomatoes, and Pesto***

*Thai Pesto***

*Arugula, Sun-Dried Tomatoes, and Goat Cheese***

*Broccoli and Aged Cheddar Cheese***

Spicy-Sweet Broccoli

*Cauliflower with Swiss Cheese and Mustard***

Golden Leek and Prosciutto Sauté

*Baby Spinach, Walnuts, Sun-Dried Tomatoes, and Feta***

*Kale and Caramelized Onions***

*Potatoes, Onions, and Gorgonzola***

*Truffled Potatoes***

*Southwestern Garbanzo Beans with Tomatoes**

*Creamy Basil Pesto***

*Mild Basil-Pecan Pesto***

*Toasted Garlic Pesto***

*Southwestern Cilantro Pesto with Green Chilies and Pumpkin Seeds***

*Kalamata Olive Tapenade with Feta and Chopped Tomato**

*Eggs Primavera***

MARINARA WITH FENNEL AND FRESH HERBS

Bulb fennel, finocchio *in Italian, has a refreshing anise flavor that makes this variation on classic marinara a delightful change of pace. You'll find the bulbs in most well-stocked supermarket produce sections and greengrocers.*

Serve with thin to medium-width strands such as angel hair, spaghettini, or spaghetti.

¼ cup extra-virgin olive oil

2 cloves garlic, chopped fine

1 small onion, chopped fine

1 small fennel bulb, stalk and root ends trimmed, tough outer layers removed, remaining bulb quartered and cut crosswise into ¼-inch-thick slices

1 28-ounce can crushed tomatoes

¼ cup finely shredded fresh basil leaves

2 tablespoons finely chopped fresh oregano leaves

1 tablespoon double-concentrate tomato paste

1 tablespoon sugar

2 bay leaves

¾ pound pasta

Salt

White pepper

Bring a large pot of water to a boil.

As soon as you put the pot over the heat, start cooking the sauce. In a large skillet or saucepan, heat the olive oil with the garlic and onion over medium heat. As soon as the garlic and onion sizzle, add the sliced fennel and sauté just until it begins to turn translucent, 2 to 3 minutes.

Add the tomatoes, basil, oregano, tomato paste, sugar, and bay leaves and stir well. Bring to a boil, reduce the heat to maintain a brisk simmer, and cook until the sauce is thick, 15 to 20 minutes.

About halfway through the sauce's simmering, add the pasta to the boiling water and cook until al dente, following the manufacturer's suggested cooking time.

Before the pasta is done, taste the sauce and add salt and white pepper to taste; remove the bay leaves. As soon as the pasta is done, drain it and toss with the sauce. Serve immediately.

SERVES 4 TO 6

ROMA TOMATOES WITH PESTO AND FRESH MOZZARELLA

This is one of my favorite elaborations on the basic pesto sauce on page 7. The contrasts of colors, flavors, and textures are wonderfully vibrant. Feel free to substitute any sun-ripened tomato for the Roma tomatoes and to vary the quantity of tomato to your personal taste. You may also substitute regular packaged mozzarella for the fresh variety.

Serve with spaghetti or linguine or other medium-width strands or ribbons.

¾ pound pasta

2 cups classic basil pesto sauce (page 7)

6 Roma tomatoes, cored and chopped coarse

½ pound fresh mozzarella cheese, drained well and cut into ½-inch cubes

Bring a large pot of water to a boil. Add the pasta and cook until al dente, following the manufacturer's suggested cooking time.

While the pasta cooks, prepare the pesto sauce. As soon as the pasta is done, drain it and toss with the pesto, tomatoes, and mozzarella cubes. Serve immediately.

SERVES 4 TO 6

Fresh Tomatoes, Mint, and Ricotta

Fresh mint gives this quick sauce a wonderfully refreshing character.

Serve with spaghetti, linguine, or other thin to medium-width strands.

¾ pound pasta

6 tablespoons extra-virgin olive oil

2 shallots, chopped fine

1½ pounds Roma tomatoes, cored and chopped coarse

½ tablespoon sugar

3 tablespoons finely chopped fresh mint leaves

Salt

Black pepper

½ pound fresh ricotta cheese, at room temperature

Bring a large pot of water to a boil. Add the pasta and cook until al dente, following the manufacturer's suggested cooking time.

While the pasta cooks, heat the olive oil and shallots in a large frying pan over medium-high heat. As soon as the shallots sizzle, add the tomatoes and sugar and sauté until the tomatoes' juices have thickened but remain fairly fluid, 5 to 7 minutes. Stir in the mint and season to taste with salt and pepper.

As soon as the pasta is done, drain it and add the sauce. With your fingers, drop in the ricotta in small clumps. Toss well and serve immediately.

Serves 4 to 6

TOMATO-ONION SAUCE WITH PROSCIUTTO AND MOZZARELLA

Although the flavors are distinctively Italian, I find that this quick sauce has all the satisfying qualities of a bacon, lettuce, and tomato sandwich! You can find the Italian salt-cured raw ham known as prosciutto in any well-stocked supermarket or Italian delicatessen; substitute good-quality ham or bacon if you cannot find it.

Serve with small to medium-sized macaroni or shells.

¾ pound pasta

6 tablespoons extra-virgin olive oil

2 cloves garlic, chopped fine

2 onions, chopped coarse

1 pound Roma tomatoes, cored and chopped coarse

6 ounces very thinly sliced prosciutto, cut into ¼-inch-wide strips

½ tablespoon sugar

½ pound fresh mozzarella cheese, cut into ½-inch cubes

6 tablespoons thinly shredded fresh basil leaves

Salt

Black pepper

Bring a large pot of water to a boil. Add the pasta and cook until al dente, following the manufacturer's suggested cooking time.

While the pasta cooks, heat the olive oil in a large skillet over medium-high heat. Add the garlic and onion and sauté until the onion is translucent, 2 to 3 minutes. Stir in the tomatoes, prosciutto, and sugar and sauté until the tomatoes' juices have thickened but are still fairly fluid, 4 to 5 minutes more. For the last minute or so of cooking, add the mozzarella and basil, stirring occasionally until the mozzarella just begins to melt but still remains in distinct cubes. Season to taste with salt and pepper.

As soon as the pasta is done, drain it and toss with the sauce. Serve immediately.

SERVES 4 TO 6

SPICY TOMATO WITH FRESH GOAT CHEESE

Tomatoes and goat cheese complement each other beautifully, the sweet, slightly acid flavor of the former playing foil to the latter's distinctive tang. A pinch of red pepper flakes and a scattering of fresh basil highlight both ingredients in a complex-tasting sauce that nonetheless cooks in less time than the pasta does. If you'd like a milder flavor, decrease the amount of red pepper flakes and substitute fresh ricotta for the goat cheese.

Serve with medium-sized tubes such as penne or rigatoni or with shapes such as fusilli or bow ties.

¾ pound pasta

6 tablespoons extra-virgin olive oil

4 cloves garlic, chopped fine

1½ pounds Roma tomatoes, cored and chopped coarse

½ tablespoon sugar

1 teaspoon crushed red pepper flakes

Salt

Black pepper

¼ cup finely shredded fresh basil leaves

½ pound fresh creamy goat cheese, at room temperature

Bring a large pot of water to a boil. Add the pasta and cook until al dente, following the manufacturer's suggested cooking time.

While the pasta cooks, heat the olive oil and garlic in a large frying pan over medium-high heat. As soon as the garlic sizzles, add the tomatoes, sugar, and red pepper flakes and sauté until the tomatoes' juices have thickened but remain fairly fluid, 5 to 7 minutes. Season to taste with salt and pepper and, if necessary, cover to keep warm.

As soon as the pasta is done, drain it and add the sauce and the basil. With your fingers, drop in the goat cheese in small clumps. Toss well and serve immediately.

SERVES 4 TO 6

BROILED EGGPLANT, FRESH TOMATOES, AND BASIL

With its rich, almost meaty flavor and satisfying texture, eggplant makes a terrific featured ingredient in a quick vegetarian pasta sauce. I recommend the long, slender, Asian-style eggplants now widely available today, because they tend to have fewer seeds and lack the edge of bitterness sometimes found in larger globe eggplants; but smaller varieties of the latter may also be used.

❧ *This chunky sauce goes very well with bite-sized tubes such as rigatoni or penne, with medium-sized shells, or with other pasta shapes.*

½ cup extra-virgin olive oil

1 pound long, slender Asian-style or small globe eggplants, trimmed, peeled thin, and cut into ¾-inch cubes

¾ pound pasta

4 cloves garlic, chopped fine

1 pound Roma tomatoes, cored and chopped coarse

½ tablespoon sugar

¼ cup packed finely shredded fresh basil leaves

Salt

Black pepper

Preheat the broiler. Bring a large pot of water to a boil.

Put one-half of the olive oil in a mixing bowl. Add the eggplant cubes and quickly toss them with the oil to coat evenly. Put the eggplant on a broiler tray and broil until they turn golden, 2 to 3 minutes per side.

Put the pasta in the boiling water and cook until al dente, following the manufacturer's suggested cooking time.

While the pasta is boiling, heat the remaining olive oil in a large skillet over medium heat. Add the garlic and sauté about 1 minute. Add the tomatoes, sugar, and broiled eggplant, raise the heat, and sauté just until the vegetables' juices thicken, about 5 minutes. Stir in the basil and season to taste with salt and pepper.

As soon as the pasta is done, drain it and toss with the sauce. Serve immediately.

SERVES 4 TO 6

CURRIED MUSHROOM AND TOMATO

Although this sauce looks like a conventional Italian sauce, its aroma and taste immediately tell you of its exotic Indian influences. Seek out a good-quality, mild to medium-hot curry powder. A dollop of plain yogurt on each serving pleasingly tempers the spiciness and enriches the sauce.

Serve with medium-sized shapes such as shells or bow ties or with medium-width ribbons such as fettuccine.

3 tablespoons unsalted butter

3 tablespoons vegetable oil

4 cloves garlic, chopped fine

2 teaspoons finely grated peeled fresh ginger

1½ pounds button mushrooms, cut into ¼-inch-thick slices

1½ tablespoons curry powder

1 28-ounce can whole tomatoes

1 tablespoon double-concentrate tomato paste

½ tablespoon sugar

¾ pound pasta

Salt

White pepper

⅓ cup plain low-fat or nonfat yogurt

¼ cup finely chopped fresh cilantro leaves

Bring a large pot of water to a boil.

Meanwhile, in a large skillet, heat the butter and oil over medium heat. As soon as the butter has melted, add the garlic and ginger and sauté until tender, about 2 minutes. Add the mushrooms and raise the heat to high. Sauté the mushrooms until they wilt and begin to brown around the edges, 7 to 10 minutes. About 1 minute before they are done, sprinkle and stir in the curry powder.

Add the tomatoes, breaking them apart with your hands. Stir in the tomato paste and sugar. Simmer the sauce until thick, about 15 minutes.

While the sauce simmers, cook the pasta in the boiling water until al dente, following the manufacturer's suggested cooking time.

When the pasta is done, drain it, toss with the sauce, and season to taste with salt and white pepper. Distribute the pasta among individual plates or shallow bowls, top with dollops of yogurt, and garnish with cilantro. Serve immediately.

SERVES 4 TO 6

ERBED BUTTON MUSHROOM MARINARA

Pick out the smallest button mushrooms you can find to present this dish at its most delicate.

✺ *Serve with angel hair, spaghettini, spaghetti, or other delicate to thin strands.*

4 tablespoons extra-virgin olive oil

2 cloves garlic, chopped fine

1½ pounds small button mushrooms, cut into ¼-inch-thick slices

1 28-ounce can crushed tomatoes

1 tablespoon double-concentrate tomato paste

½ tablespoon sugar

2 bay leaves

¾ pound pasta

2 tablespoons finely shredded fresh basil leaves

2 tablespoons finely chopped fresh chives

2 tablespoons finely chopped fresh Italian parsley

Salt

Black pepper

Grated Parmesan cheese

Bring a large pot of water to a boil.

Meanwhile, in a large skillet, heat the olive oil over medium heat. Add the garlic and sauté about 1 minute. Add the mushrooms, raise the heat to high, and sauté, stirring frequently, until they begin to brown around the edges, 7 to 10 minutes.

Add the tomatoes, tomato paste, sugar, and bay leaves to the skillet. Simmer, stirring frequently, until the sauce is thick, about 15 minutes.

Partway through the sauce's simmering, add the pasta to the boiling water and cook until al dente, following the manufacturer's suggested cooking time.

When the pasta is almost done, remove the bay leaves from the sauce and stir in the basil, chives, and parsley. Season to taste with salt and pepper. Drain the pasta and toss with the sauce. Serve immediately, passing Parmesan for guests to add to taste.

ERVES 4 TO 6

WILD MUSHROOM AND LEEK CREAM WITH MASCARPONE

Ultraluxurious and completely vegetarian, this simple sauce relies on two ingredients that are ever more available: wild mushrooms and mascarpone.

"Wild mushroom" is, in fact, now somewhat of a misnomer, as the varieties I call for—be they oyster mushrooms, portobellos, chanterelles, shiitakes, or some other good, meaty variety—are now widely raised for commercial sale; in a pinch, feel free to substitute ordinary cultivated mushrooms.

The tangy, very thick Italian cultured cream known as mascarpone may be found in well-stocked supermarkets or Italian delicatessens; French-style crème fraîche may be substituted.

Serve with medium-width ribbons such as fettuccine or with bite-sized shapes that will hold the rich sauce well such as radiatore.

¾ pound pasta

½ cup (1 stick) unsalted butter, cut into pieces

2 leeks, white parts only, trimmed well, thoroughly washed, and cut crosswise into thin slices

2 pounds wild mushrooms (see note above), wiped clean with a damp cloth, tough stems trimmed and discarded, cut into ¼-inch-thick slices

1 teaspoon dried tarragon

1½ cups mascarpone, at room temperature

Salt

Black pepper

3 tablespoons finely chopped fresh Italian parsley

3 tablespoons finely chopped fresh chives

Grated Parmesan cheese

Bring a large pot of water to a boil. Add the pasta and cook until al dente, following the manufacturer's suggested cooking time.

Meanwhile, melt the butter in a large skillet over medium heat. Add the leeks and sauté for about 1 minute. Raise the heat to medium-high, add the mushrooms, crumble in the tarragon, and sauté, stirring continuously, until the mushrooms are tender and lightly browned, 7 to 10 minutes.

Reduce the heat to medium-low, add the mascarpone, and stir continuously until it heats through and liquefies completely. Season to taste with salt and pepper.

Drain the pasta and toss with the sauce and the parsley and chives. Serve immediately, passing Parmesan for guests to add to taste.

SERVES 4 TO 6

ARTICHOKE AND TOMATO SAUTÉ

Artichoke lovers and vegetarians alike will enjoy this robust, quick sauté, which gains in zesty flavor from using widely available bottled, marinated artichoke hearts. For a milder flavor and lower-fat results, substitute frozen or water-packed artichoke hearts.

Serve with linguine, fettuccine, or other medium-width strands or ribbons or with bite-sized shapes such as bow ties or wagon wheels.

¾ pound pasta

6 tablespoons extra-virgin olive oil

4 cloves garlic, chopped fine

6 Roma tomatoes, cored and chopped coarse

2 cups marinated artichoke hearts, drained, any whole hearts cut into bite-sized quarters or halves

¼ cup drained capers

2 teaspoons dried oregano

Salt

Black pepper

2 tablespoons finely chopped fresh Italian parsley

2 tablespoons finely shredded fresh basil leaves

Bring a large pot of water to a boil. Add the pasta and cook until al dente, following the manufacturer's suggested cooking time.

While the pasta cooks, heat the olive oil and garlic in a large frying pan over medium-high heat. As soon as the garlic sizzles, add the tomatoes, artichoke hearts, capers, and oregano, and sauté until the ingredients are heated through and the tomatoes' juices have thickened but remain fairly fluid, 5 to 7 minutes. Season to taste with salt and pepper and, if necessary, cover to keep warm.

As soon as the pasta is done, drain it and toss it with the sauce and with the parsley and basil. Serve immediately.

 SERVES 4 TO 6

SAUTÉ OF FAVA BEANS, PEAS, AND ARTICHOKES WITH FRESH RICOTTA

During the late spring and early summer months when fresh peas, fava beans, and baby artichokes may be found in produce shops and farmers' markets, try this delightful, fast sauté.

Serve with tagliatelle, fettuccine, or other thin to medium-width ribbons.

1 pound fresh fava beans in their pods, shelled, tough outer skins peeled from the beans

1 pound fresh peas in their pods, shelled

¾ pound pasta

¾ cup (1½ sticks) unsalted butter, cut into pieces

½ cup extra-virgin olive oil

2 shallots, chopped fine

1 pound fresh baby artichokes, stemmed, pared, and quartered

2 tablespoons lemon juice

2 tablespoons finely chopped fresh Italian parsley

2 tablespoons finely shredded fresh basil leaves

Salt

Black pepper

½ pound fresh ricotta cheese, at room temperature

Grated Parmesan cheese

Bring a large pot of water to a boil. Add the fava beans and peas and parboil about 2 minutes. Use a wire skimmer or slotted spoon to scoop them out of the boiling water. Set them aside.

Add the pasta to the boiling water and cook until al dente, following the manufacturer's suggested cooking time.

As soon as the pasta starts cooking, heat the butter with the olive oil and the shallots in a large skillet over medium heat. As soon as the butter has melted, add the artichokes and sauté about 5 minutes. Add the reserved fava beans and peas and continue sautéing until all the vegetables are tender, 1 to 2 minutes more. Stir in the lemon juice, parsley, and basil and season with salt and pepper to taste.

As soon as the pasta is done, drain it and toss with the vegetable mixture. With your fingers, add small clumps of ricotta; then toss gently again. Serve immediately, passing Parmesan for guests to add to taste.

Serves 4 to 6

Asparagus with Browned Butter, Lemon Zest, and Parmesan Shavings

Rich and nutty-tasting, browned butter adds a wonderful dimension of flavor to tender-crisp fresh asparagus, and both are highlighted by the sprightly taste of lemon zest. Shavings of Parmesan, cut from a block of the cheese using a cheese shaver or vegetable peeler, add the perfect final touch.

Serve over medium-width strands or ribbons such as spaghetti, linguine, or fettuccine, or with bite-sized shapes such as bow ties.

1 pound asparagus, tough ends trimmed, stalks cut diagonally into ¼-inch-thick slices

¾ pound pasta

1 cup (2 sticks) unsalted butter, cut into pieces

1 tablespoon grated lemon zest

Salt

White pepper

6 ounces block Parmesan cheese

Bring a large pot of water to a boil. Add the asparagus and cook until tender-crisp, 1 to 2 minutes. Use a sieve or skimmer to scoop the vegetable pieces out of the pot and drain them well.

Add the pasta to the boiling water and cook until al dente, following the manufacturer's suggested cooking time.

About 3 minutes before the pasta is done, melt the butter in a skillet over medium heat. Continue cooking until the butter turns a rich nut-brown color, 1 to 2 minutes more, adding the asparagus and tossing it with the butter just when the color starts to change. Remove from the heat, stir in the lemon zest, and season to taste with salt and white pepper.

As soon as the pasta is done, drain it and toss with the asparagus mixture. Divide among individual serving bowls or plates and, using a cheese shaver or swivel-bladed vegetable peeler, distribute the Parmesan in thin, wide shavings generously on top. Serve immediately.

Serves 4 to 6

ASPARAGUS, FRESH TOMATOES, AND CREAM

Here's a luscious way to enjoy the flavor and texture of fresh springtime asparagus.

🌿 *Serve with spaghetti, linguine, fettuccine, or other medium-width strands or ribbons.*

¾ pound pasta

¾ cup (1½ sticks) unsalted butter, cut into pieces

2 cloves garlic, chopped fine

1 pound asparagus, tough ends trimmed, stalks cut diagonally into ¼-inch-thick slices

8 Roma tomatoes, cored, halved, seeded, and chopped coarse

1 teaspoon sugar

1 teaspoon finely chopped fresh tarragon leaves

¼ cup heavy cream

Salt

White pepper

Bring a large pot of water to a boil. Add the pasta and cook until al dente, following the manufacturer's suggested cooking time.

As soon as the pasta starts cooking, melt the butter in a large skillet over medium heat. Add the garlic and asparagus and sauté about 2 minutes. Add the tomatoes, sugar, and tarragon, reduce the heat, and continue cooking until the asparagus is tender-crisp and the pan juices have thickened slightly, 3 to 4 minutes more.

Stir in the cream, raise the heat slightly, and simmer until the sauce has thickened again, 1 to 2 minutes more. Season to taste with salt and white pepper.

As soon as the pasta is done, drain it and toss with the sauce. Serve immediately.

ERVES 4 TO 6

Mushroom, Bacon, and Pine Nut Sauté

Ordinary cultivated mushrooms are the perfect choice for this rapidly prepared sauce. If you'd like a vegetarian version, simply leave out the bacon.

Serve with medium-width strands such as spaghetti or linguine or with medium-sized shells or other shapes.

4 strips smoked bacon, chopped coarse

1 cup (2 sticks) unsalted butter, cut into pieces

2 shallots, chopped fine

3 pounds cultivated mushrooms, cut into ¼-inch-thick slices

¾ pound pasta

½ cup half-and-half

¼ cup pine nuts, toasted (see page 7)

2 tablespoons finely shredded fresh basil leaves

2 tablespoons finely chopped fresh chives

Salt

White pepper

Grated Parmesan cheese

Bring a large pot of water to a boil.

While the water comes to a boil, cook the bacon in a large, nonstick skillet over medium heat until golden brown and crisp, about 5 minutes. Remove the bacon from the skillet and drain on paper towels. Pour off the fat from the skillet.

In the same skillet, melt the butter over medium-high heat. Add the shallots and sauté for about 1 minute.

Add the mushrooms to the skillet and sauté, raising the heat slightly and stirring frequently, until their juices reduce to a glaze, about 20 minutes.

Meanwhile, add the pasta to the boiling water and cook until al dente, following the manufacturer's suggested cooking time.

A few minutes before the pasta is done, stir the half-and-half into the mushroom mixture, raise the heat to high, and cook until it reduces to a thick sauce, 3 to 4 minutes. Stir in the reserved bacon and the pine nuts, basil, and chives and season to taste with salt and white pepper.

As soon as the pasta is done, drain it and toss with the sauce. Serve immediately, passing Parmesan for guests to add to taste.

Serves 4 to 6

SHIITAKE MUSHROOM AND GARLIC SAUTÉ

Not so long ago an exotic Asian specialty, dark brown, meaty-tasting shiitake mushrooms have become widely available in the produce sections of well-stocked supermarkets. They're so satisfying that even confirmed carnivores find this quick sauce a nice change of pace.

Serve with fettuccine or other medium-width ribbons.

½ cup (1 stick) unsalted butter, cut into pieces

4 cloves garlic, chopped fine

1 pound fresh shiitake mushrooms, tough stems trimmed and discarded, caps cut into ¼-inch-thick slices

¾ pound pasta

¼ cup heavy cream

1 tablespoon soy sauce

½ tablespoon lemon juice

White pepper

Salt

2 tablespoons finely chopped fresh Italian parsley

2 tablespoons finely chopped fresh chives

2 tablespoons pine nuts, toasted (see page 7)

Bring a large pot of water to a boil.

While the water comes to a boil, melt the butter in a large skillet over medium heat. Add the garlic and, as soon as it gives off an aroma, stir in the mushrooms. Sauté, stirring frequently, until the mushrooms begin to turn golden brown, 7 to 10 minutes.

Meanwhile, put the pasta in the boiling water and cook until al dente, following the manufacturer's suggested cooking time.

Stir the cream, soy sauce, and lemon juice into the mushroom mixture and continue cooking until the liquid reduces to a thick sauce, 3 to 5 minutes more. Season to taste with white pepper and, if necessary, a little salt.

As soon as the pasta is done, drain it and toss with the sauce and the parsley, chives, and pine nuts. Serve immediately.

 SERVES 4 TO 6

Asparagus, Shiitake Mushrooms, Sun-Dried Tomatoes, and Pesto

For a quick and elegant meal, try this luxurious elaboration on a basic pesto sauce. Fresh shiitake mushrooms may be found in many well-stocked supermarkets, produce shops, and farmers' markets, but regular cultivated mushrooms may be substituted.

Serve with medium-width ribbons such as tagliatelle or fettuccine or with medium-sized tubes or shapes such as penne or bow ties.

¾ pound pasta

¼ cup extra-virgin olive oil

¾ pound asparagus, ends trimmed, cut diagonally into ¼-inch-thick slices

½ pound fresh shiitake mushrooms, stems cut off and discarded, caps cut into ¼-inch-thick slices

½ cup drained oil-packed sun-dried tomatoes, cut into thin slivers

1 cup classic basil pesto sauce (recipe on page 7)

Bring a large pot of water to a boil. Add the pasta and cook until al dente, following the manufacturer's suggested cooking time.

About halfway through the pasta's cooking time, heat the olive oil in a large skillet over high heat. Add the asparagus and mushrooms and sauté until the asparagus is barely tender-crisp, 3 to 4 minutes. Add the sun-dried tomatoes and sauté about 1 minute more.

As soon as the pasta is done, drain it and toss with the asparagus mixture and the pesto. Serve immediately.

Serves 4 to 6

THAI PESTO

Lovers of Thai food will find this simple, almost instantaneously made pasta sauce irresistible. If you like, top it with some quickly grilled shrimp that you've briefly marinated in a little lemon or lime juice, soy sauce, and vegetable oil.

Serve with thin to medium-width strands or ribbons such as angel hair, spaghettini, linguine, or tagliatelle, or with freshly boiled chow mein noodles.

¾ pound pasta

1¼ cups peanut or vegetable oil

1 cup packed fresh basil leaves, stems removed

1 cup packed fresh cilantro leaves

1 cup packed fresh mint leaves

1 cup grated Parmesan cheese

¼ cup Asian-style toasted sesame oil

¾ cup dry-roasted peanuts

3 cloves garlic, peeled

Bring a large pot of water to a boil. Add the pasta and cook until al dente, following the manufacturer's suggested cooking time.

Put all the remaining ingredients in a food processor fitted with the metal blade. Turning the machine on and off rapidly, pulse the ingredients several times until chopped coarse. Scrape down the work bowl. Then process continuously until the sauce is smooth. If the pesto seems too thick, pulse in a little boiling water from the pasta.

As soon as the pasta is done, drain it and toss with the pesto. Serve immediately.

SERVES 4 TO 6

Arugula, Sun-Dried Tomatoes, and Goat Cheese

The flavors of this rapid pasta sauce are as vivid as its colors. You'll find refreshingly bitter arugula leaves, also known as rocket, in the produce sections of well-stocked supermarkets as well as in good greengrocers and farmers' markets. I recommend using oil-packed sun-dried tomatoes for this recipe, as using reconstituted air-packed sun-dried tomatoes will cause splattering when you add them to the hot oil. You can use some of the tomatoes' flavorful packing oil as part of the measure of olive oil in the sauce.

Serve with fine to medium-width strands such as angel hair, spaghettini, spaghetti, or linguine.

¾ pound pasta

1 cup extra-virgin olive oil

2 cloves garlic, chopped fine

¾ cup oil-packed drained sun-dried tomatoes, cut into ¼-inch-wide pieces

1 cup packed whole arugula leaves

½ pound fresh creamy goat cheese, at room temperature

Salt

Black pepper

Bring a large pot of water to a boil. Add the pasta and cook until al dente, following the manufacturer's suggested cooking time.

When the pasta is almost done, heat the olive oil and garlic in a large frying pan over medium heat. As soon as the garlic sizzles, reduce the heat to low and add the sun-dried tomatoes; cook until they are heated through, 1 to 2 minutes more.

As soon as the pasta is done, drain it and add the sun-dried tomato mixture and the arugula leaves. With your fingers, drop in the goat cheese in small clumps. Season to taste with salt and pepper. Toss well and serve immediately.

Serves 4 to 6

BROCCOLI AND AGED CHEDDAR CHEESE

There's a natural affinity between broccoli and cheddar that has long made them natural side-dish partners and works equally well in a quick pasta sauce. A sharp aged cheddar stands up better to the vegetable's strong taste, and one with a good, deep yellow-orange color provides a prettier contrast.

❧ *Serve with bite-sized pasta shapes such as wagon wheels or bow ties.*

6 cups packed small broccoli florets

¾ pound pasta

2 tablespoons unsalted butter

½ small onion, chopped very fine

3 cups heavy cream

1½ pounds aged sharp cheddar cheese, shredded

½ cup grated Parmesan cheese

4 drops hot pepper sauce, such as Tabasco

Salt

White pepper

Bring a large pot of water to a boil. Add the broccoli and cook until barely tender-crisp, 2 to 3 minutes. Use a skimmer or large slotted spoon to lift the broccoli from the water and set it aside. Add the pasta to the water and cook until al dente, following the manufacturer's suggested cooking time.

As soon as the pasta starts cooking, melt the butter in a saucepan over medium heat. Add the onion and sauté until it begins to turn translucent, about 2 minutes. Add the cream, raise the heat to medium-high, and bring to a boil. Reduce the heat to very low and, stirring continuously, sprinkle in the shredded cheddar and then the Parmesan. When the cheese has melted completely and thickened the sauce, add the hot pepper sauce and then season to taste with salt and white pepper.

Put the broccoli pieces in the sauce and continue simmering gently to heat the broccoli through, 1 to 2 minutes.

When the pasta is done, drain it and toss immediately with the sauce.

 ERVES 4 TO 6

SPICY-SWEET BROCCOLI

It's surprising how well the taste of broccoli goes with other assertively flavored ingredients like the red pepper flakes, sweet raisins, and salty anchovy that flavor this unusual sauce.

Serve with bite-sized shapes such as radiatore or bow ties.

2 tablespoons seedless golden raisins

2 cups bite-sized broccoli florets

¾ pound pasta

¼ cup extra-virgin olive oil

¼ cup (½ stick) unsalted butter

2 cloves garlic, chopped fine

½ teaspoon crushed red pepper
   flakes

4 canned anchovy fillets, chopped
   fine

Salt

Black pepper

Bring a large pot of water to a boil.

Put the raisins in a small heatproof bowl. With a ladle, carefully pour just enough of the boiling water over them to cover them completely. Leave to soak.

Put the broccoli in the pot of boiling water and cook until tender-crisp, 4 to 5 minutes. Use a wire skimmer or slotted spoon to lift out the broccoli and set it aside.

Add the pasta to the boiling water and cook until al dente, following the manufacturer's suggested cooking time.

As soon as the pasta starts cooking, heat the olive oil and butter in a large skillet over medium-low heat. Add the garlic and red pepper flakes and cook about 1 minute. Reduce the heat and stir in the anchovies, mashing them with a wooden spoon to dissolve them.

Drain the raisins well and add them to the skillet along with the broccoli. Cook, stirring, until the mixture is heated through, 1 to 2 minutes more.

As soon as the pasta is done, drain it, toss with the sauce, and season to taste with salt and pepper. Serve immediately.

SERVES 4 TO 6

CAULIFLOWER WITH SWISS CHEESE AND MUSTARD

I am one of the many people who usually find cauliflower unpalatable when it's unadorned. But I love it when the vegetable's cabbagey nature is softened through a pairing with rich, tangy, nutlike Swiss cheese, or with a cream sauce, or when it is seasoned with equally pungent mustard. All three of these improvements join together in this quick sauce.

Serve with bite-sized pasta shapes such as wagon wheels or bow ties.

6 cups packed cauliflower florets

¾ pound pasta

3 cups heavy cream

1½ pounds Swiss, Gruyère, or Emmenthaler cheese, shredded

½ cup grated Parmesan cheese

2 teaspoons grainy Dijon-style mustard

Salt

White pepper

4 tablespoons finely chopped fresh chives

Bring a large pot of water to a boil. Add the cauliflower and cook until tender-crisp, 3 to 4 minutes. Use a skimmer or large slotted spoon to lift the cauliflower from the water and set it aside.

Add the pasta to the water and cook until al dente, following the manufacturer's suggested cooking time.

As soon as the pasta starts cooking, bring the cream to a boil in a saucepan over medium-high heat. Reduce the heat to very low and, stirring continuously, sprinkle in the shredded cheese and then the Parmesan. When the cheeses have melted completely and thickened the sauce, stir in the mustard until it blends in completely. Then season to taste with salt and white pepper.

Put the cauliflower florets in the sauce and continue simmering gently to heat the cauliflower through, 1 to 2 minutes.

When the pasta is done, drain it and toss immediately with the sauce. Garnish with chives and serve at once.

SERVES 4 TO 6

GOLDEN LEEK AND PROSCIUTTO SAUTÉ

The mild flavor of the leek, a relative of the onion, gains in sweetness when it is sautéed to a caramel brown color. Italian prosciutto adds its own savor, making this a dish as beguiling as it is simple to prepare.

> *Serve with medium-width strands such as spaghetti or linguine or medium-sized shapes such as shells or bow ties.*

½ cup (1 stick) unsalted butter, cut into pieces

½ cup extra-virgin olive oil

5 leeks, white parts only, trimmed, split lengthwise, washed thoroughly, and cut into ¼-inch-thick slices

¾ pound pasta

4 ounces thinly sliced prosciutto, cut into ¼-by-1-inch strips

2 tablespoons finely chopped fresh Italian parsley

Grated Parmesan cheese

Bring a large pot of water to a boil.

Meanwhile, melt the butter with the olive oil in a large skillet over medium heat. Add the leeks and sauté until they turn golden brown, 10 to 12 minutes.

After the leeks start cooking, put the pasta in the boiling water and cook until al dente, following the manufacturer's suggested cooking time.

A minute or so before the leeks are done, stir in the prosciutto.

As soon as the pasta is done, drain it and toss with the prosciutto mixture. Garnish with parsley and serve immediately, passing Parmesan for guests to add to taste.

Serves 4 to 6

Baby Spinach, Walnuts, Sun-Dried Tomatoes, and Feta

There's something so casually Mediterranean about this combination that with each bite, you can close your eyes and almost imagine yourself on a sunny terrace. Be sure to use oil-packed sun-dried tomatoes. Many markets today sell packaged bags of fresh, washed and dried baby spinach leaves; take advantage of them if they're available.

✑ *Serve with medium-width ribbons such as fettuccine or with bite-sized shapes such as wagon wheels, fusilli, or bow ties.*

¾ pound pasta

1 cup (2 sticks) unsalted butter, cut into pieces

2 cloves garlic, chopped fine

1 cup shelled walnut pieces

½ cup drained oil-packed sun-dried tomatoes, cut into ¼-inch-wide strips

Pinch of nutmeg

2 cups packed whole baby spinach leaves, washed if necessary and patted thoroughly dry

½ pound feta cheese, crumbled

Salt

Black pepper

Bring a large pot of water to a boil. Add the pasta and cook until al dente, following the manufacturer's suggested cooking time.

A few minutes before the pasta is done, melt the butter in a large skillet over medium heat. Add the garlic and sauté for about 1 minute. Then, add the walnuts and sauté until they darken slightly in color and smell toasty, about 1 minute more.

Add the sun-dried tomatoes to the skillet and sauté until they are heated through, about 1 minute. Sprinkle in the smallest pinch of nutmeg. Finally, just before the pasta is done, add the spinach and stir continuously just until the leaves barely begin to wilt, about 30 seconds more.

Drain the pasta and toss with the sauce and the crumbled feta cheese, seasoning to taste with salt and pepper. Serve immediately.

Serves 4 to 6

KALE AND CARAMELIZED ONIONS

If you've never tried kale, you can't begin to imagine how good this simple, rustic combination of the robust greens and caramelized onions can be. The few drops of hot pepper sauce I suggest add an extra dimension of rich flavor without making the dish taste perceptibly spicy, but go ahead and leave it out if you're at all wary of Tabasco and its ilk. If you're not strictly vegetarian, feel free to include an ounce or two of thinly sliced, coarsely chopped bacon, pancetta, or prosciutto sautéed along with the onion.

Serve with bite-sized shapes such as wagon wheels, bow ties, or radiatore or with medium-sized shells.

6 tablespoons extra-virgin olive oil

1 large onion, chopped coarse

1 tablespoon sugar

2 bunches kale (about 2 dozen medium-sized to large leaves)

¾ pound pasta

4 to 6 drops hot pepper sauce, such as Tabasco

Salt

Black pepper

Grated Parmesan

Put the olive oil and onion in a large pot and cook over medium heat, stirring frequently, until the onion begins to turn a light golden color, 5 to 7 minutes. Sprinkle in the sugar and cook, stirring continuously until the onion turns a deep caramel brown color, 5 to 7 minutes more.

While the onion cooks, prepare the kale leaves. Rinse each leaf thoroughly under cold running water; do not dry them. Snap off the tough parts of the stems and discard. Bunch together several leaves at a time and, with a sharp knife, cut carefully across the bunch at ½-inch intervals to make bite-sized strips. Set aside.

When the onion is browned, add the kale to the pot with the moisture still clinging to it. Stir with a wooden spoon to mix the onion with the kale and pack the kale down into the pot. Reduce the heat to low, cover securely, and cook until the kale is fairly tender, 30 to 45 minutes, stirring occasionally. The kale will reduce considerably in volume.

While the kale cooks, bring another large pot filled with water to a boil. About 10 minutes or so before the kale is done, add the pasta to the water and cook until al dente, following the manufacturer's suggested cooking time.

Stir hot pepper sauce into the kale mixture to taste. Season with salt and pepper. As soon as the pasta is done, drain it and toss with the sauce. Serve immediately, passing Parmesan for guests to add.

$\mathcal{S}$ERVES 4 TO 6

POTATOES, ONIONS, AND GORGONZOLA

What a wonderfully robust pasta dish this recipe makes! It becomes even easier if you start with boiled potatoes left over from a previous night's dinner. It's especially good if you use some of the buttery-tasting, yellow-fleshed potatoes now available, such as Yukon Gold or Yellow Finn. For the gorgonzola, you may substitute any other blue cheese that might be available.

Serve with bite-sized shapes such as bow ties or radiatore.

1 pound small to medium-sized
  boiling potatoes, cut into
  ½-inch-thick slices

4 tablespoons (½ stick) unsalted
  butter

2 tablespoons extra-virgin olive oil

1 medium-sized to large onion,
  chopped coarse

¾ pound pasta

Salt

Black pepper

½ pound gorgonzola cheese,
  crumbled

¼ cup finely chopped fresh chives

Bring a large pot of water to a boil. Add the potatoes and cook until barely tender when tested with the tip of a small, sharp knife, about 10 minutes.

Meanwhile, melt one-half of the butter with one-half of the olive oil in a large skillet over medium-low heat. Add the onion and sauté while the potatoes cook.

As soon as the potatoes are ready, use a wire skimmer or slotted spoon to remove them from the water. Drain well on paper towels.

Add the pasta to the boiling water and cook until al dente, following the manufacturer's suggested cooking time.

Meanwhile, add the remaining butter and oil to the skillet along with the potatoes and sauté the potatoes and onion together until the onion begins to turn caramel brown and the potatoes golden, about 10 minutes. Season to taste with salt and pepper.

As soon as the pasta is done, drain it and toss with the potato mixture and the gorgonzola and chives. Serve immediately.

SERVES 4 TO 6

TRUFFLED POTATOES

Think of this pasta sauce combination of diced potatoes and truffle-scented olive oil as heaven and earth. They go well together. You'll find small bottles of this precious, wondrously scented olive oil in specialty food stores.

Serve with bite-sized shapes such as bow ties, fusilli, or radiatore.

1 pound small to medium-sized boiling potatoes, cut into ½-inch dice

6 tablespoons unsalted butter

2 shallots, chopped fine

¾ pound pasta

½ cup truffle-scented olive oil

Salt

Black pepper

¼ cup finely chopped fresh chives

Bring a large pot of water to a boil. Add the potatoes and cook until barely tender when tested with the tip of a small, sharp knife, about 10 minutes.

Meanwhile, melt the butter in a large skillet over medium-low heat. Add the shallots and sauté about 1 minute. Set aside.

As soon as the potatoes are ready, use a wire skimmer or slotted spoon to remove them from the water. Drain well on paper towels.

Add the pasta to the boiling water and cook until al dente, following the manufacturer's suggested cooking time.

Meanwhile, add the potatoes to the skillet and sauté until they begin to turn golden, about 10 minutes. Stir in the truffle-scented olive oil and cook until heated, about 1 minute more. Season to taste with salt and pepper.

As soon as the pasta is done, drain it and toss with the sauce and the chives. Serve immediately.

Serves 4 to 6

SOUTHWESTERN GARBANZO BEANS WITH TOMATOES

Robust spicing makes this quick sauce a satisfying pasta topping.

Serve with bite-sized shapes such as wagon wheels or radiatore or with medium-sized shells.

4 tablespoons extra-virgin olive oil

4 cloves garlic, chopped fine

2 small fresh hot green chilies such as serranos, stemmed, seeded, and chopped fine

1 onion, chopped fine

½ tablespoon cumin

½ tablespoon cayenne pepper

1 28-ounce can crushed tomatoes

2 8¾-ounce cans garbanzo beans (chickpeas), drained

1 tablespoon double-concentrate tomato paste

½ tablespoon sugar

½ tablespoon dried oregano

¾ pound pasta

Salt

Black pepper

Hot pepper sauce, such as Tabasco

¼ cup finely chopped fresh cilantro leaves

Bring a large pot of water to a boil.

Meanwhile, in a large skillet or saucepan, heat the olive oil over medium heat. Add the garlic, chilies, and onion and sauté until the onion turns translucent, 2 to 3 minutes. Add the cumin and cayenne pepper and sauté about 1 minute more.

Add the tomatoes, garbanzo beans, tomato paste, sugar, and oregano. Stir and scrape the bottom of the pan with a wooden spoon to dissolve any of the spices adhering to it. Simmer briskly until thick, 15 to 20 minutes.

Partway through the sauce's simmering, add the pasta to the boiling water and cook until al dente, following the manufacturer's suggested cooking time.

Season the sauce to taste with salt, black pepper, and a few drops of hot pepper sauce. As soon as the pasta is done, drain it and toss with the sauce and the cilantro. Serve immediately.

SERVES 4 TO 6

CREAMY BASIL PESTO

Some simple changes to the classic Genovese sauce—replacing the olive oil with half-and-half and adding just a touch of butter—produce a wonderfully different version of pesto. Try this in place of the classic basil pesto recipe on page 7.

Serve with delicate to medium-width strands or ribbons such as angel hair, spaghetti, linguine, tagliatelle, or fettuccine.

¾ pound pasta

3 cups packed fresh basil leaves, stems removed

¾ cup pine nuts, toasted (see page 7)

2 cloves garlic, peeled

1 cup grated Parmesan cheese

1 cup half-and-half

¼ cup (½ stick) unsalted butter, at room temperature

Bring a large pot of water to a boil. Add the pasta and cook until al dente, following the manufacturer's suggested cooking time.

Meanwhile, put the basil, pine nuts, and garlic in a food processor fitted with the metal blade. Pulse the machine on and off until the ingredients are mixed and coarsely chopped.

Add the Parmesan, half-and-half, and butter and process just until the mixture is well blended, stopping if necessary to scrape down the work bowl.

If the pesto seems too thick, pulse in just a splash of boiling water from the pasta.

As soon as the pasta is done, drain it and toss with the pesto. Serve immediately.

SERVES 4 TO 6

MILD BASIL-PECAN PESTO

Some people find the bite of a classic basil pesto (page 7) a little too strong. Here's a good, equally quick sauce to ease them into the pesto experience. It doesn't even require extra-virgin olive oil (though you can use it if you wish); rather, it calls for pure olive oil, which does not have so pronounced a flavor.

Serve with delicate to medium-width strands or ribbons such as angel hair, spaghetti, tagliatelle, or fettuccine.

¾ pound pasta

1½ cups pure olive oil

1½ cups packed fresh Italian parsley

1½ cups packed fresh basil leaves, stems removed

1 cup grated Parmesan cheese

¾ cup shelled pecan pieces, toasted (see page 7)

1 or 2 cloves garlic, peeled

Bring a large pot of water to a boil. Add the pasta and cook until al dente, following the manufacturer's suggested cooking time.

Put the olive oil, parsley, basil, Parmesan, pecans, and garlic in a food processor fitted with the metal blade. Turning the machine on and off rapidly, pulse the ingredients several times until chopped coarse. Scrape down the work bowl. Then process continuously until the sauce is smooth. If the pesto seems too thick, pulse in a little boiling water from the pasta.

As soon as the pasta is done, drain it and toss with the pesto. Serve immediately.

 SERVES 4 TO 6

TOASTED GARLIC PESTO

Think of this as garlic lovers' pesto, free of herbs. Simmering the garlic in milk before cooking it takes out all its harshness.

Serve with medium-width strands or ribbons such as spaghetti, tagliatelle, or fettuccine.

8 cloves garlic, peeled and sliced thin
   lengthwise

1 cup milk

¾ pound pasta

1 cup extra-virgin olive oil

1 cup pine nuts, toasted (see page 7)

1 cup grated Parmesan cheese

Bring a large pot of water to a boil.

While the water is coming to a boil, put the garlic and ½ cup of the milk in the smallest saucepan you have. Bring to a boil over medium heat. Drain and discard the milk. Add the remaining ½ cup milk to the pan, bring to a boil again, and then drain and pat the garlic completely dry with paper towels.

Add the pasta to the boiling water and cook until al dente, following the manufacturer's suggested cooking time.

Meanwhile, put the garlic and ¼ cup of the olive oil in a small skillet. Sauté the garlic over medium heat until it turns golden brown, 3 to 5 minutes.

Put the remaining ¾ cup olive oil and the pine nuts and Parmesan in a food processor fitted with the metal blade. Then add the garlic and its cooking oil. Turning the machine on and off rapidly, pulse the ingredients several times until chopped coarse. Scrape down the work bowl and process continuously until the sauce is smooth. If the pesto seems too thick, pulse in a little boiling water from the pasta.

As soon as the pasta is done, drain it and toss with the pesto. Serve immediately.

SERVES 4 TO 6

SOUTHWESTERN CILANTRO PESTO WITH GREEN CHILIES AND PUMPKIN SEEDS

Scan the ingredients and you'll see that this unusual pesto follows the same logic as a classic Genovese version, with its fresh herbs, nuts, cheese, olive oil, and garlic. All the ingredients are easily found in a well-stocked supermarket. If you can't find the crumbly white Mexican-style cheese known as queso fresco, *substitute a mild feta. This is also good as a base for chicken breasts that have been quickly grilled as in the recipe on page 42.*

Serve with medium-width strands or ribbons such as spaghetti, linguine, tagliatelle, or fettuccine.

¾ pound pasta

1½ cups extra-virgin olive oil

1½ cups packed fresh cilantro leaves

1 cup packed fresh Italian parsley

½ cup drained canned roasted mild green chilies

½ cup pine nuts, toasted (see page 7)

¼ cup shelled pumpkin seeds, toasted (see page 7)

1 cup *queso fresco* or mild feta cheese, crumbled

3 cloves garlic, peeled

Bring a large pot of water to a boil. Add the pasta and cook until al dente, following the manufacturer's suggested cooking time.

Put all the remaining ingredients in a food processor fitted with the metal blade. Turning the machine on and off rapidly, pulse the ingredients several times until chopped coarse. Scrape down the work bowl. Then process continuously until the sauce is smooth. If the pesto seems too thick, pulse in a little boiling water from the pasta.

As soon as the pasta is done, drain it and toss with the pesto. Serve immediately.

SERVES 4 TO 6

KALAMATA OLIVE TAPENADE WITH FETA AND CHOPPED TOMATO

Tapenade, the quickly blended Provençale dip, gets an Aegean twist in this recipe, which partners an aromatic paste of briny Greek black olives with sweet pieces of ripe tomato and small cubes of the eastern Mediterranean's pungent Greek sheep's milk cheese. You'll find Kalamata olives sold by weight in the deli cases of well-stocked supermarkets, as well as in jars; some brands may be found already pitted. Substitute any other brine-cured Mediterranean olives you like.

Serve with spaghetti, linguine, tagliatelle, or other medium-width strands or ribbons.

¾ pound pasta

1 pound Kalamata olives, pitted (about 2 cups)

1 cup extra-virgin olive oil

2 large cloves garlic

½ cup packed fresh Italian parsley

¼ cup drained capers

2 tablespoons lemon juice

1 tablespoon dried oregano

¾ pound feta cheese, crumbled or cut into ¼- to ½-inch cubes

4 large Roma tomatoes, halved, cored, seeded, and cut into ¼- to ½-inch pieces

Bring a large pot of water to a boil. Add the pasta to the water and cook until al dente, following the manufacturer's suggested cooking time.

While the pasta cooks, put the olives, olive oil, garlic, parsley, capers, lemon juice, and oregano in a food processor fitted with the metal blade. Turning the machine on and off rapidly, pulse the ingredients a few times, then scrape down the work bowl and process continuously until the mixture forms a coarse but uniform paste.

As soon as the pasta is done, drain it and immediately toss with the tapenade and one-half of the feta and one-half of the tomatoes. Top with the remaining feta and tomatoes and serve immediately.

SERVES 4 TO 6

EGGS PRIMAVERA

Scrambling pasta with eggs and cream makes a deliciously satisfying dish that you can serve as easily for breakfast or brunch as for dinner. Here, the preparation is prettily elaborated with a mixture of finely shredded or diced vegetables.

🌿 *Serve with spaghetti or linguine.*

¾ pound pasta

8 eggs

¼ cup half-and-half or light cream

½ cup grated Parmesan cheese

6 tablespoons unsalted butter

2 shallots, chopped fine

¼ cup coarsely shredded carrot

¼ cup thinly sliced mushrooms

2 Roma tomatoes, cored, halved, seeded, and cut into ¼-inch dice

2 tablespoons finely chopped fresh Italian parsley

2 tablespoons finely chopped fresh chives

2 tablespoons finely shredded fresh basil leaves

Black pepper

Bring a large pot of water to a boil. Add the pasta and cook until al dente, following the manufacturer's suggested cooking time.

Meanwhile, in a mixing bowl, lightly beat the eggs. Beat in the half-and-half and the Parmesan. Set aside.

In a large skillet, melt the butter over medium-low heat. Add the shallots and sauté about 1 minute. Add the carrot and mushrooms and sauté until they are heated through, 1 to 2 minutes more. Stir in the tomatoes.

As soon as the pasta is done, drain it and add it to the skillet, tossing briefly to mix it with the vegetable mixture. Pour the egg mixture over the pasta and cook, stirring and tossing the entire mixture gently, until the egg forms creamy curds that coat the pasta and vegetables. Shortly before the mixture is finished cooking, sprinkle in the parsley, chives, and basil. Season to taste with pepper and serve immediately.

SERVES 4 TO 6

Dairy and Oil Sauces

Herbed Ricotta and Butter**

Eggs with Goat Cheese and Sun-Dried Tomatoes**

Creamy Goat Cheese with Garlic and Fresh Basil**

Brie and Parmesan with Slivered Almonds**

Smoked Mozzarella and Hazelnuts**

Tomato Alfredo**

Four-Cheese Pizzaiola**

Golden Parmesan Butter**

Parmesan and Pine Nut Toss**

Garlic-Parmesan Butter**

* This recipe is vegan; that is, it contains no animal products whatsoever.
** This recipe uses dairy or eggs but no other animal products.

Fines Herbes Butter**

Red Chili Butter**

Seeded Butter**

Hazelnut Butter**

Butter and Cinnamon Sugar**

Butter, Olive Oil, Scallions, Garlic, and Fresh Herbs**

Olive Oil with Frizzled Parsley**

Aglio e Olio Arrabiata*

Vegetarian Carbonara**

HERBED RICOTTA AND BUTTER

I think of this dish as a perfect example of Italian comfort food. It combines the earthiness of pasta, the fluffy richness of fresh ricotta, and the bright green colors and delicate flavors of commonly available fresh herbs. Seek out fresh ricotta, which has a lighter texture and flavor, in Italian delicatessens and specialty food stores; regular packaged ricotta will also work well, however.

Serve with medium-sized ribbons such as fettuccine, with medium-sized shapes such as rotelli or bow ties, or with medium-sized shells.

¾ pound pasta

1 cup (2 sticks) unsalted butter, cut into pieces

2 pounds ricotta cheese, at room temperature, drained

2 tablespoons finely shredded fresh basil leaves

2 tablespoons finely chopped fresh chives

2 tablespoons finely chopped fresh Italian parsley

Salt

Black pepper

Bring a large pot of water to a boil. Add the pasta and cook until al dente, following the manufacturer's suggested cooking time.

About 1 minute before the pasta is done, melt the butter in a medium-sized skillet or saucepan over medium heat. As soon as the pasta is done, drain it and toss with the melted butter. With your fingertips, add the ricotta in small clumps. Add the herbs, toss well, and season to taste with salt and pepper. Serve immediately.

SERVES 4 TO 6

EGGS WITH GOAT CHEESE AND SUN-DRIED TOMATOES

This breakfast pasta combination features two of the most popular, intense flavors of nouvelle cuisine. You'll find both goat cheese and sun-dried tomatoes today in well-stocked supermarkets or gourmet delicatessens.

Serve with spaghetti or linguine.

¾ pound pasta

8 eggs

¼ cup half-and-half or light cream

½ cup grated Romano cheese

¼ cup (½ stick) unsalted butter, cut into pieces

2 cloves garlic, chopped fine

½ cup drained oil-packed sun-dried tomatoes, cut into ½-inch-wide strips

6 ounces fresh creamy goat cheese

¼ cup finely shredded fresh basil leaves

Black pepper

Bring a large pot of water to a boil. Add the pasta and cook until al dente, following the manufacturer's suggested cooking time.

Meanwhile, in a mixing bowl, lightly beat the eggs. Beat in the half-and-half and the Romano. Set aside.

Melt the butter in a large skillet over medium-low heat. Add the garlic and sauté for about 1 minute. Drain the pasta and add it to the skillet, tossing briefly to mix it with the butter and garlic. Pour the egg mixture over the pasta and cook, stirring and tossing the entire mixture gently, until the egg begins to thicken and coat the pasta. Add the sun-dried tomatoes and, with your fingertips, drop in small clumps of the goat cheese. Continue cooking until the cheese melts and the eggs form moist curds that cling to the pasta. Add the basil and season to taste with pepper during the last moments of cooking.

Serve immediately.

SERVES 4 TO 6

CREAMY GOAT CHEESE
WITH GARLIC AND FRESH BASIL

When you toss these quickly prepared ingredients with hot pasta, you'll be amazed by the wonderful, heady aromas.

Serve with thin to medium-width strands or ribbons such as angel hair, spaghetti, or linguine.

¾ pound pasta

¼ pound (1 stick) unsalted butter, cut into pieces

2 to 4 cloves garlic, chopped fine

1½ pounds fresh creamy goat cheese, at room temperature

6 tablespoons finely shredded fresh basil leaves

Bring a large pot of water to a boil. Add the pasta to the boiling water and cook until al dente, following the manufacturer's suggested cooking time.

While the pasta cooks, melt the butter in a medium-sized saucepan over medium-low heat. Add the garlic and sauté until it turns translucent, 2 to 3 minutes. Remove from the heat and set aside.

When the pasta is done, drain it and immediately toss with the butter and garlic. With your fingertips, quickly add small clumps of the soft goat cheese to the pasta. Then add the basil and toss again. Serve at once.

SERVES 4 TO 6

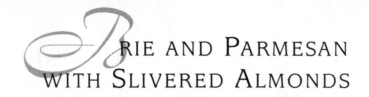

BRIE AND PARMESAN WITH SLIVERED ALMONDS

This recipe was inspired by a party hors d'oeuvre that was very popular a few years back, in which a whole wheel of ripe Brie was studded with almonds and baked until the nuts turned toasty and the cheese became molten. Not a bad idea for a pasta sauce!

Serve with fettuccine or other medium-width ribbons.

¾ pound pasta

1½ cups heavy cream

¾ pound ripe Brie, rind cut off, at room temperature

1 cup grated Parmesan cheese

½ cup slivered almonds, toasted (see page 7)

2 tablespoons finely chopped fresh chives

2 tablespoons finely chopped fresh Italian parsley

Bring a large pot of water to a boil. Add the pasta and cook until al dente, following the manufacturer's suggested cooking time.

Meanwhile, bring the cream to a boil in a heavy saucepan over medium heat. Reduce the heat to low. With your fingertips, break off small clumps of Brie and carefully drop them into the cream. Stir until it melts and blends with the cream. Then, sprinkle in the Parmesan, stirring until it, too, blends in and the sauce thickens.

As soon as the pasta is done, drain it and toss with the sauce and the toasted almonds. Serve immediately, garnished with chives and parsley.

SERVES 4 TO 6

Smoked Mozzarella and Hazelnuts

When it is smoked, mozzarella develops a firmer texture and a rich, aromatic flavor with just an edge of sweetness. I find that chopped, toasted hazelnuts add a complementary flavor and crunch.

Serve with medium-width ribbons such as fettuccine or tagliatelle or with bite-sized shapes such as fusilli, bow ties, or wagon wheels.

¾ pound pasta

¾ cup (1½ sticks) unsalted butter, cut into pieces

¾ cup hazelnuts, toasted (see page 7), skins rubbed off, nuts coarsely chopped

1 cup heavy cream

¾ pound smoked mozzarella cheese, shredded coarse

Salt

White pepper

2 tablespoons finely chopped fresh chives

Bring a large pot of water to a boil. Add the pasta and cook until al dente, following the manufacturer's suggested cooking time.

About halfway through the pasta's cooking time, melt the butter in a large skillet over medium-high heat. Add the hazelnuts and, as soon as the butter begins to foam, stir in the cream. Bring to a brisk simmer. Just moments before the pasta is done, stir in the mozzarella and remove the skillet from the heat.

As soon as the pasta is done, drain it and toss with the sauce, seasoning to taste with salt and white pepper. Garnish with chives and serve immediately.

Serves 4 to 6

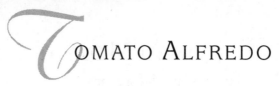

TOMATO ALFREDO

Adding a little chopped fresh tomato and a dollop of tomato paste to a classic Alfredo sauce transforms it into a sauce of a different color, with a rosy hue and a beguilingly sweet edge of extra flavor.

Serve with regular or green fettuccine or any other medium-width ribbons.

¾ pound pasta

¾ cup (1½ sticks) unsalted butter, cut into pieces

1½ cups heavy cream

2 tablespoons double-concentrate tomato paste

¾ cup grated Parmesan cheese

½ cup grated Romano cheese

3 Roma tomatoes, stemmed, halved, seeded, and cut into ¼-inch dice

4 tablespoons finely shredded fresh basil leaves

Bring a large pot of water to a boil. Add the pasta and cook until al dente, following the manufacturer's suggested cooking time.

Meanwhile, in a medium-sized saucepan, heat the butter and cream over medium heat, stirring occasionally, until the butter melts and the cream is hot. Stir in the tomato paste until it dissolves. Gradually stir in the Parmesan and Romano until they have melted and thickened the sauce.

As soon as the pasta is done, drain it and toss with the sauce and the tomatoes. Garnish with the basil and serve immediately.

ERVES 4 TO 6

Four-Cheese Pizzaiola

The combination of cheeses, garlic, tomatoes, and herbs in this sauce conjures sensations of a classic pizza. If you feel so inclined, you may stir in a handful of chopped sliced pepperoni sausage or even a few minced anchovies shortly before serving to achieve your own pizza-style ideal.

Serve with medium-width ribbons such as fettuccine or tagliatelle.

¾ pound pasta

2 tablespoons unsalted butter

2 cloves garlic, chopped fine

2 cups heavy cream

¼ pound fontina cheese, shredded

¼ pound fresh creamy goat cheese,
  cut into small pieces

½ cup grated Parmesan cheese

½ cup grated Romano cheese

4 Roma tomatoes, cored and
  chopped coarse

1 teaspoon dried oregano

1 teaspoon dried basil

Bring a large pot of water to a boil. Add the pasta and cook until al dente, following the manufacturer's suggested cooking time.

While the pasta cooks, melt the butter in a medium-sized saucepan over medium heat. Add the garlic and sauté about 1 minute. Add the cream and, as soon as it is hot but before it starts to boil, stir in the fontina and the goat cheese.

As the cheeses begin to melt, raise the heat slightly and bring the sauce to a boil, stirring constantly. Reduce the heat and simmer the sauce gently until it is thick and creamy, 3 to 5 minutes. A minute or so before it is done, add the Parmesan and Romano cheeses and the tomatoes and, with your fingertips, crumble in the oregano and basil. Stir well.

As soon as the pasta is done, drain it, toss it with the sauce, and serve immediately.

Serves 4 to 6

GOLDEN PARMESAN BUTTER

I've always loved the nutty flavor cheese acquires when it has cooked to a golden brown color. This variation on one of the simplest of pasta sauces, melted butter and grated Parmesan, develops added depth of flavor by cooking the ingredients together briefly in a skillet until they take on a rich hue. Be sure to use a good-quality imported Italian Parmesan that has been freshly grated either by yourself at home or at the deli section of the market that sells it.

 *Serve with medium-width strands or ribbons such as spaghetti, linguine, or fettuccine.*

¾ pound pasta

1 cup unsalted butter, cut into pieces

1 cup grated Parmesan cheese

Salt

Black pepper

Bring a large pot of water to a boil. Add the pasta and cook until al dente, following the manufacturer's suggested cooking time.

About 3 minutes before the pasta is done, melt the butter in a medium-sized nonstick skillet over medium heat. When the butter begins to foam, sprinkle and stir in the Parmesan and continue cooking until both the butter and the cheese take on a light golden color, about 1 minute more. Keep a close eye on the mixture to guard against overcooking and burning.

As soon as the pasta is done, drain it and toss with the Parmesan mixture. Season to taste with salt and pepper and serve immediately.

Serves 4 to 6

PARMESAN AND PINE NUT TOSS

One of the most classic, simple and quick pasta treatments is to toss it with melted butter and Parmesan cheese. Replacing part of the cheese with coarsely chopped pine nuts adds yet another rich dimension of flavor.

Serve with spaghetti, linguine, or other thin to medium-width strands.

¾ pound pasta

½ cup pine nuts, toasted (see page 7)

¾ cup (1½ sticks) unsalted butter, melted

½ cup grated Parmesan cheese

2 tablespoons finely chopped fresh chives

2 tablespoons finely chopped fresh Italian parsley

Bring a large pot of water to a boil. Add the pasta and cook until al dente, following the manufacturer's suggested cooking time.

Meanwhile, put the pine nuts in a food processor fitted with the metal blade. Pulse the machine a few times, just until the pine nuts are chopped coarse.

As soon as the pasta is done, drain it and add the melted butter and the pine nuts and the Parmesan, chives, and parsley. Toss well and serve immediately.

Serves 4 to 6

GARLIC-PARMESAN BUTTER

The very same sort of butter mixture that you would spread on a split Italian loaf to make garlic bread works wonderfully as a superfast pasta sauce that needs no cooking at all. If you don't have a food processor to blend the mixture, use a garlic press to puree the garlic cloves and then, in a bowl, use a fork to mash them together with the softened butter before mashing in the cheese.

❧ *Serve with spaghetti, linguine, tagliatelle, fettuccine, or other common strands or ribbons.*

¾ pound pasta

4 cloves garlic, peeled

1 cup unsalted butter, cut into
    pieces, at room temperature

1 cup grated Parmesan cheese

Salt

Black pepper

Bring a large pot of water to a boil. Add the pasta and cook until al dente, following the manufacturer's suggested cooking time.

While the pasta cooks, prepare the garlic-Parmesan butter. First, put the garlic cloves in a food processor fitted with the metal blade. Turning the machine on and off rapidly, pulse until the garlic is chopped fine, stopping once or twice to scrape down the work bowl. Add the butter and the Parmesan and pulse the ingredients briefly until they are blended smooth. Scrape the butter mixture out of the bowl and set it aside.

As soon as the pasta is done, drain it and immediately toss with the garlic-Parmesan butter and season to taste with salt and pepper. Serve immediately.

Serves 4 to 6

FINES HERBES BUTTER

If you have easy access to fresh fines herbes from a window box, a garden, a greengrocer, or a farmers' market, this lovely, prettily scented pasta dish couldn't be simpler or quicker to make.

Serve with medium-width strands or ribbons such as spaghetti, linguine, or fettuccine.

¾ pound pasta

¾ cup (1½ sticks) unsalted butter, cut into pieces

2 tablespoons finely shredded fresh basil leaves

2 tablespoons finely chopped fresh chives

2 tablespoons finely chopped fresh Italian parsley

½ tablespoon finely chopped fresh tarragon leaves

Salt

White pepper

Grated Parmesan cheese

Bring a large pot of water to a boil. Add the pasta and cook until al dente, following the manufacturer's suggested cooking time.

Just before the pasta is done, melt the butter in a medium-sized skillet over medium heat.

As soon as the pasta is done, drain it and toss with the butter and the herbs. Season to taste with salt and white pepper. Serve immediately, passing Parmesan for guests to add to taste.

SERVES 4 TO 6

RED CHILI BUTTER

A dash of dried red chili powder turns simple pasta with butter into an intriguing Southwestern treat. Use pure powdered dried red chili for this recipe, steering clear of chili powder mixtures meant for chili con carne, which contain several other seasonings besides the chili itself. You'll find it in the spice aisles or ethnic food sections of well-stocked supermarkets. The powder commonly comes in several different strengths. Unless you know well the heat tolerance of you and your guests, try this recipe first with a mild or medium-hot pure red chili powder.

 *Serve with spaghetti, linguine, or other medium-width strands or ribbons.*

¾ pound pasta

1 cup (2 sticks) unsalted butter, cut into pieces

1 teaspoon pure red chili powder

Salt

White pepper

Grated Parmesan cheese

Bring a large pot of water to a boil. Add the pasta and cook until al dente, following the manufacturer's suggested cooking time.

About 3 minutes before the pasta is done, put the butter in a medium-sized skillet over medium heat. As soon as the butter begins to melt, sprinkle in the red chili powder and continue cooking until the butter is completely melted and the red chili butter gives off a full, rich aroma, 1 to 2 minutes more.

As soon as the pasta is done, drain it and toss with the red chili butter mixture. Season to taste with salt and white pepper. Serve immediately, passing Parmesan for guests to add to taste.

*S*ERVES 4 TO 6

SEEDED BUTTER

If you enjoy breads that contain the wonderful taste and texture embellishments of sesame or poppy seeds, then you'll love this made-in-a-minute pasta sauce. I like it with a mixture of seeds, but feel free to use all of one or the other if you like.

The sauce is especially good with medium-width to wide ribbons such as fettuccine or pappardelle and with any sort of egg noodle.

¾ pound pasta

1½ cups (3 sticks) unsalted butter, cut into pieces

½ cup mixed sesame and poppy seeds

Salt

White pepper

Grated Parmesan cheese

Bring a large pot of water to a boil. Add the pasta and cook until al dente, following the manufacturer's suggested cooking time.

A few minutes before the pasta is done, melt the butter in a large skillet over medium-low heat. Add the seeds and sauté, stirring continuously, until the seeds darken slightly in color and give off a nutlike aroma, no more than 1 minute.

The moment the pasta is done, drain and toss it with the seeded butter and season to taste with salt and white pepper. Serve immediately, passing Parmesan for guests to add to taste.

SERVES 4 TO 6

HAZELNUT BUTTER

Hazelnuts are my favorite nut, and a simple butter sauce and freshly grated Parmesan show off their rich flavor and crunchiness to wonderful effect.

Serve with medium-width strands such as spaghetti or linguine.

1 cup hazelnuts, toasted (see page 7), skins rubbed off

¾ pound pasta

1 cup (2 sticks) unsalted butter, cut into pieces

1 cup grated Parmesan cheese

As soon as the hazelnuts have cooled, put them in a food processor fitted with the metal blade. Turning the machine on and off quickly, pulse the hazelnuts several times, stopping the moment they are chopped very coarse. Set them aside.

Bring a large pot of water to a boil. Add the pasta and cook until al dente, following the manufacturer's suggested cooking time.

A few minutes before the pasta is done, put the butter in a skillet or saucepan and melt over medium heat. Add the hazelnuts and sauté, stirring continuously, until they are heated through, 1 minute more.

The moment the pasta is done, toss it with the hazelnut butter and the Parmesan. Serve immediately.

ERVES 4 TO 6

BUTTER AND CINNAMON SUGAR

Quick comfort food, this dish is incredibly satisfying as a special breakfast treat. In fact, it's a delightful indulgence when you're all alone, so try dividing the quantities by four!

Serve with small pasta shapes, from little shells to macaroni to orzo, or egg noodles.

¾ pound pasta

¾ cup (1½ sticks) unsalted butter, cut into pieces

¼ cup packed light brown sugar

½ teaspoon ground cinnamon

Bring a large pot of water to a boil. Add the pasta and cook until al dente, following the manufacturer's suggested cooking time.

Just before the pasta is done, melt the butter in a large skillet over medium heat. Sprinkle in the brown sugar and the cinnamon and turn the heat to low.

As soon as the pasta is done, drain it, add it to the skillet and toss with the sauce. Serve immediately.

SERVES 4 TO 6

Butter, Olive Oil, Scallions, Garlic, and Fresh Herbs

Simple ingredients and quick cooking yield a wonderfully aromatic little pasta sauce that also delights with its bright green flecks of color.

❧ *Serve with spaghetti or linguine.*

¾ pound pasta

½ cup (1 stick) unsalted butter, cut into pieces

½ cup extra-virgin olive oil

4 scallions, trimmed and cut crosswise into thin slices

4 cloves garlic, chopped fine

2 tablespoons finely chopped fresh chives

2 tablespoons finely chopped fresh Italian parsley

Salt

White pepper

Grated Parmesan cheese

Bring a large pot of water to a boil. Add the pasta and cook until al dente, following the manufacturer's suggested cooking time.

A few minutes before the pasta is done, melt the butter with the olive oil in a large skillet over medium heat. Add the scallions and garlic and sauté just until the scallions have wilted and both the scallions and garlic give off a rich fragrance, 1 to 2 minutes.

As soon as the pasta is done, drain it and toss with the scallion mixture and the parsley and chives. Season to taste with salt and white pepper. Serve immediately, passing Parmesan for guests to add to taste.

Serves 4 to 6

OLIVE OIL
WITH FRIZZLED PARSLEY

Parsley that has been fried briefly in olive oil acquires an intriguing flavor and a wonderfully crisp edge of texture. After you've rinsed the parsley and before you chop it, be sure to dry it thoroughly with a dish towel or paper towels to prevent its splattering. Also take care not to overcook the parsley.

Serve with spaghetti, linguine, or other medium-width strands.

¾ pound pasta

1 cup extra-virgin olive oil

½ cup coarsely chopped fresh
   Italian parsley

Salt

Black pepper

Grated Parmesan cheese

Bring a large pot of water to a boil. Add the pasta and cook until al dente, following the manufacturer's suggested cooking time.

About 2 minutes before the pasta is done, heat the olive oil in a large skillet over medium-high heat. Add the parsley and sauté, stirring continuously, just until it turns a deeper green color, 30 seconds to 1 minute. Keep a close eye on the parsley to guard against overcooking and burning.

As soon as the pasta is done, drain it and toss with the parsley and season to taste with salt and pepper. Serve immediately, passing Parmesan for guests to add to taste.

SERVES 4 TO 6

AGLIO E OLIO ARRABIATA

The classically simple sauce of garlic and extra-virgin olive oil, known by the Italian aglio e olio, *gains an exciting—or "rabid"—new facet by including a sprinkling of the crushed red pepper flakes to be found in the spice section of any supermarket.*

Serve with medium-width strands. Spaghetti is most traditional, but linguine would be good as well.

¾ pound pasta

1½ cups extra-virgin olive oil

8 cloves garlic, chopped fine

1 to 2 teaspoons crushed red pepper flakes

Salt

Black pepper

Bring a large pot of water to a boil. Add the pasta and cook until al dente, following the manufacturer's suggested cooking time.

A few minutes before the pasta is done, heat the olive oil in a large skillet over medium heat. Add the garlic and sauté just until it turns light golden, 1 to 2 minutes. Stir in the red pepper flakes and sauté until they release their aroma, about 30 seconds more.

Drain the pasta and toss with the sauce. Season to taste with salt and pepper. Serve immediately, passing Parmesan for guests to add to taste.

SERVES 4 TO 6

VEGETARIAN CARBONARA

It's a shame that devoted vegetarians miss out on one of the most pleasurable of all pasta preparations because of the bacon included in the classic version of the Italian "charcoal maker's" sauce. This recipe aims to capture the original recipe's bacony flavor through the addition of a little smoked cheese.

Serve with spaghetti.

¾ pound pasta

4 tablespoons unsalted butter

2 cloves garlic, chopped fine

6 egg yolks

2 cups heavy cream

2 cups grated Parmesan cheese

½ pound smoked mozzarella
    cheese, shredded coarse

Freshly ground black pepper

¾ cup finely chopped fresh
    Italian parsley

Bring a large pot of water to a boil. Add the pasta and cook until al dente, following the manufacturer's suggested cooking time.

Meanwhile, melt the butter in a large skillet. Add the garlic and sauté about 1 minute. Set aside.

In a bowl, beat the egg yolks, cream, and 1½ cups of the Parmesan.

As soon as the pasta is done, drain it and add to the skillet. Pour in the cream mixture and toss over low heat for about 1 minute. Add the mozzarella and continue tossing until the sauce thickens and coats the pasta, 1 to 2 minutes more. Sprinkle generously with the remaining Parmesan and the pepper and parsley. Serve immediately.

SERVES 4 TO 6

INDEX

Aglio e Olio (oil and garlic) Arrabiata, 126
Anchovy
    Butter, 21
    Butter, Spicy, with Roasted Garlic, 26
    Pissaladière, 27
Artichoke(s)
    Fava Beans, and Peas with Fresh Ricotta, Sauté of, 83
    and Tomato Sauté, 82
    and Tomatoes, Turkey Sausage with, 57
Arugula
    Steak with, Cherry Tomatoes and Creamy Dressing, 58
    Sun-Dried Tomatoes, and Goat Cheese, 90
    Sun-Dried Tomatoes, and Parmesan, Roast Chicken with, 49
and Tomato Cream, Grilled Salmon with, 30
Asparagus
    with Browned Butter, Lemon Zest, and Parmesan Shavings, 84
    Fresh Tomatoes, and Cream, 85
    Shiitake Mushrooms, Sun-Dried Tomatoes, and Pesto, 88

Bacon, Canadian, and Smoked Chicken, Eggs with, 41
Bacon, Mushroom, and Pine Nut Sauté, 86
Basil-Pecan Pesto, Mild, 102
Basil Pesto, Creamy, 101
Beans. *See* Fava Beans; Garbanzo Beans
Beef (Sauce), 58–61
    Chili Sundae, 60
    and Sausage Bolognese, 61
    and Shiitake Mushroom Bolognese, 59

Steak with Cherry Tomatoes, Arugula, and Creamy Dressing, 58
Bolognese (Sauce)
    Beef and Sausage, 61
    Beef and Shiitake Mushroom, 59
    Greek, with Lamb, Eggplant, Kalamata Olives, and Feta, 68
    Ground Chicken, with Fines Herbes, 46
    Sausage, Creamy, 62
    Turkey, Mexican, 54
Brie (Cheese)
    Grilled White Sausage with, and Dijon Cream Sauce, 67
    and Parmesan with Slivered Almonds, 112
    and Sweet Sausage, Eggs with, 64
Broccoli
    and Aged Cheddar Cheese, 91
    Goat Cheese, Sun-Dried Tomatoes, and Garlic, Sautéed Chicken with, 48
    Spicy Sweet, 92
Butter (Sauce), 109–24
    and Cinnamon Sugar, 123
    Fines Herbes, 119
    Garlic Parmesan, 118
    Hazelnut, 122
    Herbed Ricotta and, 109
    Olive Oil, Scallions, Garlic, and Fresh Herbs, 124
    Parmesan, Golden, 116
    Parmesan and Pine Nut Toss, 117
    in pasta sauces, 6
    Red Chili, 120
    Seeded (poppy and sesame), 121

Canadian Bacon and Smoked Chicken, Eggs with, 41

Caponata, Tuna, 35

Cauliflower with Swiss Cheese and Mustard, 93

Caviar, Golden, Smoked Salmon, Smoked Trout, and
    Lemon-Orange Butter, 34

Cheddar Cheese, Aged, Broccoli and, 91

Cheese *See also* Name of Cheese
    in pasta sauces, 6
    Pizzaiola, Four-, 115

Chicken (Sauce), 41–52. *See also* Turkey
    Alfredo, Grilled, 42
    Breasts, Grilled, with Red Bell Pepper–Sun-Dried
        Tomato Pesto, 44
    Ground, Bolognese with Fines Herbes, 46
    Ground, and Pine Nut Meatballs with Lemon Butter,
        47
    Roast, with Arugula, Sun-Dried Tomatoes, and
        Parmesan, 49
    Roast, and Chicken Sausage with Tomatoes and
        Mascarpone, 52
    Sautéed, with Broccoli, Goat Cheese, Sun-Dried
        Tomatoes, and Garlic, 48
    Smoked, Eggs with, and Canadian Bacon, 41

Chicken Livers, Prosciutto, and Shiitake Mushrooms with
    Marsala Cream, 50

Chili Butter, Red, 120

Chili Sundae (beef, pork), 60

Cilantro Pesto with Green Chilies and Pumpkin Seeds,
    Southwestern, 104

Cinnamon Sugar and Butter, 123

Clam Sauce, Quick White, with Pancetta, 23

Clams, Spicy Steamed, with Fresh Tomatoes and Garlic, 22

Coconut Cream, Mussels with, 24

Crab, Spicy and Zesty, 20

cream in pasta sauces, 6

Curried Mushroom and Tomato, 79

Dairy (Sauce). *See* Butter; Name of Cheese

Eggplant, Broiled, Fresh Toamtoes, and Basil, 78

Eggplant, Lamb, Kalamata Olives, and Feta, Greek Bolognese
    with, 68

Eggs
    with Goat Cheese and Sun-Dried Tomatoes, 110
    in pasta sauces, 7
    Primavera, 106
    with Smoked Chicken and Canadian Bacon, 41
    with Sweet Sausage and Brie, 64

Fava Beans, Peas, and Artichokes with Fresh Ricotta, Sauté
    of, 83

Fennel and Fresh Herbs, Marinara with, 73

Feta (Cheese)
    Baby Spinach, Walnuts, Sun-Dried Tomatoes and, 95
    Greek Bolognese with Lamb, Eggplant, Kalamata Olives,
        and, 68
    Kalamata Olive Tapenade with Chopped Tomato and,
        105

Fines Herbes Butter, 119

Fish (Sauce). *See* Seafood

Four-Cheese Pizzaiola, 115

Garbanzo Beans with Tomatoes, Southwestern, 100

Garlic
    Aglio e Olio Arrabiata, 126
    Butter, Olive Oil, Scallions, Fresh Herbs and, 124
    Chicken, Sautéed, with Broccoli, Goat Cheese, Sun-
        Dried Tomatoes and, 48
    Creamy Goat Cheese with Fresh Basil and, 111
    –Herb Cheese, Smoked Salmon with, 33
    -Parmesan Butter, 118
    in pasta sauces, 7
    Pesto, Toasted, 103

Roasted, Spicy Anchovy Butter with, 26

and Shiitake Mushroom Sauté, 87

Spicy Steamed Clams with Fresh Tomatoes and, 22

Tuna, Olives, Fresh Herbs, and, 36

Goat Cheese

Arugula, Sun-Dried Tomatoes, and, 90

Broccoli, Sun-Dried Tomatoes, Garlic, and Sautéed
Chicken with, 48

Creamy, with Garlic and Fresh Basil, 111

Fresh, Spicy Tomato with, 77

and Sun-Dried Tomatoes, Eggs with, 110

and Sun-Dried Tomatoes, Smoked Turkey with, 56

Gorgonzola (Cheese), Potatoes, Onions, and, 98

Greek Bolognese with Lamb, Eggplant, Kalamata Olives, and
Feta, 68

Green Chilies and Pumpkin Seeds, Southwestern Cilantro
Pesto with, 104

Grilled

Chicken Alfredo, 42

Chicken Breasts with Red Bell Pepper–Sun-Dried
Tomato Pesto, 44

Lamb Tenderloin with Pistachio-Mint Pesto, 70

Salmon with Tomato Cream and Arugula, 30

Scallops with Ginger-Soy Butter, 19

Scallops with Pancetta and Sun-Dried Tomatoes, 18

Shrimp with Ginger Champagne Cream and Caviar, 16

Shrimp with Lime-Ginger Butter, 14

White Sausage with Brie and Dijon Cream Sauce, 67

Ham. See also Pancetta; Prosciutto

with Vegetable Streamers, 66

Hazelnut Butter, 122

Hazelnuts, Smoked Mozzarella and, 113

Herbed Button Mushroom Marinara, 80

Herbed Ricotta and Butter, 109

herbs in pasta sauces, 7

Kalamata Olive Tapenade with Feta and Chopped Tomato,
105

Kale and Caramelized Onions, 96

Lamb, Eggplant, Kalamata Olives, and Feta, Greek Bolognese
with, 68

Lamb, Grilled, Tenderloin with Pistachio-Mint Pesto, 70

Leek, Golden, and Prosciutto Sauté, 94

Leek and Wild Mushroom Cream with Mascarpone, 81

Marinara with Fennel and Fresh Herbs, 73

Marinara, Herbed Button Mushroom, 80

Mascarpone (Cheese), Roast Chicken and Chicken Sausage
with Tomatoes, and, 52

Mascarpone, Wild Mushroom and Leek Cream with, 81

Meat Sauce. See Name of Meat (beef, lamb, pork, etc.)

Mexican Turkey Bolognese, 54

Mozzarella (Cheese)

Fresh, Roma Tomatoes with Pesto and, 74

Smoked, and Hazelnuts, 113

Tomato-Onion Sauce with Prosciutto and, 76

Mushroom. See also Shiitake; Wild Mushroom

Bacon, and Pine Nut Sauté, 86

Button, Marinara, Herbed, 80

Curried, and Tomato, 79

Mussels with Coconut Cream, 24

nuts in pasta sauces, 7

Olive Oil

Aglio e Olio Arrabiata, 126

Butter, Scallions, Garlic, and Fresh Herbs, 124

with Frizzled Parsley, 125

in pasta sauces, 8

Olive Tapenade, Kalamata, with Feta and Chopped Tomato,
105

Olives, Tuna, Garlic, and Fresh Herbs, 36
Onion-Tomato Sauce with Prosciutto and Mozzarella, 76
Onions, Carmelized, and Kale, 96

Pancetta
    with Onions, Tomatoes, and Parmesan, 65
    Quick White Clam Sauce with, 23
    and Sun-Dried Tomatoes, Grilled Scallops with, 18
Parmesan (Cheese)
    and Brie with Slivered Almonds, 112
    Butter, Golden, 116
    Garlic-Butter, 118
    and Pine Nut Toss, 117
    Shavings, Asparagus with Browned Butter, Leon Zest
        and, 84
Parsley, Frizzled, Olive Oil with, 125
pasta
    cooking guide, 5; cooking times, 6
    al dente, 5
    pantry items for sauces, 6–9
    shapes of, guide to, 1–4
Peas, Fava Beans, and Artichokes with Fresh Ricotta, Sauté
    of, 83
Peas, Spring, Tuna with, 38
peppers in pasta sauces, 8
Pesto
    Asparagus, Shiitake Mushrooms, Sun-Dried Tomatoes
        and, 88
    Basil, Creamy, 101
    Basil-Pecan, Mild, 102
    Cilantro, with Green Chiles and Pumpkin Seeds,
        Southwestern, 104
    Pistachio-Mint, Grilled Lamb Tenderloin with, 70
    Red Bell Pepper–Sun-Dried Tomato, Grilled Chicken
        Breasts with, 44
    Roma Tomatoes with, and Fresh Mozzarella, 74

Thai (herb), 89
Toasted Garlic, 103
Pine Nut and Ground Chicken Meatballs with Lemon Butter,
    47
Pistachio-Mint Pesto, Grilled Lamb Tenderloin with, 70
Pizzaiola, Four Cheese, 115
Pork (Sauce). See also Bacon; Ham; Pancetta; Sausage Chili
    Sundae, 60
Potatoes, Onions, and Gorgonzola, 98
Potatoes, Truffled, 99
Prosciutto
    Chicken Livers, and Shiitale Mushrooms with Marsala
        Cream, 50
    and Golden Leek Sauté, 94
    Tomato-Onion Sauce with Mozarella and, 76

Red Bell Pepper-Sun-Dried Tomato Pesto, Grilled Chicken
    Breasts with, 44
Red Chili Butter, 120
Ricotta (Cheese)
    Fresh, Fava Beans, Peas, and Artichokes with, Sauté of,
        83
    Fresh Tomatoes, Mint, and, 75
    Herbed, and Butter, 109

Salmon. See also Smoked Salmon
    Grilled, with Tomato Cream and Arugula, 30
Sardines, Tomato, and Fresh Dill, 28
sauces, pantry items for, 6–9
Sausage
    and Beef Bolognese, 61
    Bolognese, Creamy, 62
    Chicken, and Roast Chicken with Tomatoes and
        Mascarpone, 52
    Chunky Sweet, with Tomato-Chili Cream, 63
    Sweet, Eggs with, and Brie, 64

Turkey, with Artichokes and Tomatoes, 57
White, Grilled, with Brie and Dijon Cream Sauce, 67
Scallops, Grilled, with Ginger-Soy Butter, 19
Scallops, Grilled, with Pancetta and Sun-Dried Tomatoes, 18
Seafood (Sauce), 13–38
Anchovy Butter, 21
Anchovy Butter, Spicy, with Roasted Garlic, 26
Anchovy Pissaladière, 27
Clam, Quick White, with Pancetta, 23
Clams, Spicy Steamed, with Fresh Tomatoes and Garlic, 22
Crab, Spicy and Zesty, 20
Mussels with Coconut Cream, 24
Salmon, Grilled, with Tomato Cream and Arugula, 30
Sardines, Tomato, and Fresh Dill, 28
Scallops, Grilled, with Ginger-Soy Butter, 19
Scallops, Grilled, with Pancetta and Sun-Dried Tomatoes, 18
Shrimp, Baby Bay, with Bacon and Chives, 15
Shrimp, Baby Bay, with Lemon-Dill Butter, 13
Shrimp, Grilled, with Ginger Champagne Cream and Caviar, 16
Shrimp, Grilled, with Lime-Ginger Butter, 14
Smoked Salmon with Garlic-Herb Cheese, 33
Smoked Salmon, Roma Tomatoes, Capers, and Lemon Zest, 29
Smoked Salmon, Smoked Trout, Golden Caviar, and Lemon-Orange Butter, 34
Smoked Salmon with Vodka Cream, 32
Tuna Caponata, 35
Tuna with Celery, 37
Tuna, Olives, Garlic, and Fresh Herbs, 36
Tuna with Spring Peas, 38
Seeded (poppy and sesame) Butter, 121
shallots in pasta sauces, 8
Shiitake Mushroom. See also Mushroom; Wild Mushroom

Asparagus, Sun-Dried Tomatoes, and Pesto, 88
and Beef Bolognese, 59
Chicken Livers, and Prosciutto with Marsala Cream, 50
and Garlic Sauté, 87
Shrimp
Baby Bay, with Bacon and Chives, 15
Baby Bay, with Lemon-Dill Butter, 13
Grilled, with Ginger Champagne Cream and Caviar, 16
Grilled, with Lime-Ginger Butter, 14
Smoked Chicken and Canadian Bacon, Eggs with, 41
Smoked Mozzarella and Hazelnuts, 113
Smoked Salmon
with Garlic-Herb Cheese, 33
Roma Tomatoes, Capers, and Lemon Zest, 29
Smoked Trout, Golden Caviar, and Lemon-Orange Butter, 34
with Vodka Cream, 32
Smoked Trout, Smoked Salmon, Golden Caviar, and Lemon-Orange Butter, 34
Smoked Turkey with Goat Cheese and Sun-Dried Tomatoes, 56
Southwestern Cilantro Pesto with Green Chilies and Pumpkin Seeds, 104
Southwestern Garbanzo Beans with Tomatoes, 100
Spinach, Baby, Walnuts, Sun-Dried Tomatoes, and Feta, 95
Steak with Cherry Tomatoes, Arugula, and Creamy Dressing, 58
Sun-Dried Tomato(es)
Arugula, and Goat Cheese, 90
Arugula, and Parmesan, Roast Chicken with, 49
Asparagus, Shiitake Mushrooms, and Pesto, 88
Baby Spinach, Walnuts, and Feta, 95
Broccoli, Goat Cheese, and Garlic, Sautéed Chicken with, 48
Eggs with Goat Cheese and, 110
and Goat Cheese, Smoked Turkey with, 56

and Pancetta, Grilled Scallops with, 18
in pasta sauces, 9
–Red Bell Pepper Pesto, Grilled Chicken Breasts with, 44
Swiss Cheese, Cauliflower with, and Mustard, 93

Thai (herb) Pesto, 89
Tomato(es)
    Alfredo, 114
    and Artichoke Sauté, 82
    Asparagus, and Cream, Fresh, 85
    -Chili Cream, Chunky Sweet Sausage with, 63
    Cream and Arugula, Grilled Salmon with, 30
    and Feta, Kalamata Olive Tapenade with, 105
    Fresh, Broiled Eggplant, and Basil, 78
    Garbanzo Beans with, Southwestern, 100
    Mint, and Ricotta, Fresh, 75
    and Mushroom, Curried, 79
    -Onion Sauce with Prosciutto and Mozzarella, 76
    Roma, with Pesto and Fresh Mozzarella, 74
    Roma, Smoked Salmon, Capers, and Lemon Zest, 29
    Spicy, with Fresh Goat Cheese, 77
    and tomato paste in pasta sauce, 9
Truffled Potatoes, 99
Tuna
    Caponata, 35
    with Celery, 37
    Olives, Garlic, and Fresh Herbs, 36
    with Spring Peas, 38

Turkey (Sauce), 53–57. *See also* Chicken
    Bolognese, Mexican, 54
    Breast Piccata, 53
    Sausage with Artichokes and Tomatoes, 57
    Smoked, with Goat Cheese and Sun-Dried Tomatoes, 56

Vegan (Sauce) (no animal products)
    Aglio e Olio Arrabiata, 126
    Artichoke and Tomato Sauté, 82
    Eggplant, Broiled, Fresh Tomatoes, and Basil, 71
    Garbanzo Beans with Tomatoes, Southwestern, 72
    Marinara with Fennel and Fresh Herbs, 73
Vegetable(s) Sauce, 73–106. *See also* Name of Vegetable
    Basil-Pecan Pesto, Mild, 102
    Basil Pesto, Creamy, 101
    Eggs Primavera, 106
    Garlic Pesto, Toasted, 103
    Kalamata Olive Tapenade with Feta and Chopped Tomato, 105
    Southwestern Cilantro Pesto with Green Chilies and Pumpkin Seeds, 104
    Streamers, Ham with, 66
    Thai Pesto, 89
    Vegetarian Carbonara, 127
Vegetarian Carbonara, 127
Vegetarian Sauce. *See* Dairy and Oil Sauce; Vegetable

Wild Mushroom. *See also* Mushroom; Shiitake
    and Leek Cream with Mascarpone, 81